Praise for *Invitation to Impact*

"Wendy Steele is one of the bright lights attempting to tip this world away from negativity and division to a world that sees a viable path to optimism and positive change. Importantly, in *Invitation to Impact*, she demonstrates how we can move connection and meaning from a longing to a lifelong practice. A positive and connected brain is the greatest advantage in the modern world, but it is something we do with one another instead of alone. This book provides a practical and clear path to light the way."

—**Shawn Achor**, *New York Times* best-selling author of *Big Potential* and *The Happiness Advantage*

"Wendy has created dramatic change in the world. Impact100—her brainchild—has awarded $105 million in grants to nonprofits that are transforming communities. Her own personal story of how she came to inspire and empower women to give so generously is no less amazing."

—**Doug Stanton**, #1 *New York Times* best-selling author of *In Harm's Way* and *12 Strong*

"They say that innovation is born from necessity. Few understand this—live this—with stronger qualifications than Wendy Steele, who shares invaluable lessons which led to her standing as a philanthropic groundbreaker. The reach of Wendy's work has changed lives, and her illuminating insights will empower more women to share in her success and give back with greater impact inside their local communities."

—**Ambassador Nancy G. Brinker**, global cancer advocate, founder of Susan G. Komen for the Cure and Promise Fund of Florida

"*Invitation to Impact* is a reminder that by working together we make a much bigger impact than we can alone. As I say in all of my lectures, the small ethical decisions we make each day may seem unimportant, but if millions make the same ethical decisions this will lead to change. The time has come for global cooperation on a large scale, and Steele's book provides many stories that illustrate that such cooperation is our only hope of survival."

—**Dr. Jane Goodall, Ph.D., DBE,** founder of the Jane Goodall Institute and UN Messenger of Peace

"Wendy's life story is not just a powerful tale of resilience. It's an inspiration to all who wonder, 'What can I do to make a difference?' Buy this book, read this book, and share this book. Then, together with your friends, marvel at all the ways you can effect transformative change."

—**Angie Morgan,** entrepreneur and *New York Times* best-selling author of *SPARK*, *Leading from the Front*, and *Bet on You*

"Reading this book will introduce you to an amazing woman, Wendy Steele. Her heartfelt journey while developing a unique and overwhelmingly successful way for women to express their gratitude, while helping to solve their community's issues, is a story not to be missed. Wendy's shared experiences will help women all over the globe realize they can be a powerful force for change. This is a 'must read.'"

—**Sondra Shaw Hardy,** co-founder of the Women's Philanthropy Institute at the Lilly Center on Philanthropy at Indiana University; co-director of the Women's Philanthropy Institute when the "Women's Giving Circles" movement was launched

"A personal, practical guide to mobilizing local solutions to global problems."

—**Adam Grant,** #1 *New York Times* best-selling author of *Think Again* and host of the TED podcast *WorkLife*

"Drawing on a deep understanding of how and why women give, Impact100 founder Wendy Steele shares the tools and actions we need to create meaningful change across our communities. Both inspiring and practical, *Invitation to Impact* is a must-have guide to transformative philanthropy rooted in empathy and service."

—**Susan Spencer,** former editor-in-chief of *Woman's Day* magazine

"With an unparalleled depth of insight and clarity of voice, Wendy Steele is the voice of the generosity movement. Her speaking abilities, writing skills, and servant leadership touch a place in the hearts of generous givers on a global scale. She is a generous woman who has enriched many lives, including my own. Don't miss her wisdom and insight!"

—**Michael Chatman,** president and CEO, Global Center for Generosity at The Community Foundation

"Wendy Steele brings her visionary gift of grassroots, women-powered philanthropy to the world in *Invitation to Impact*. It's a must-read for anyone who knows they have more to give but needs a guide on their philanthropic journey. This inspiring book will change the way you think about your impact on the world."

—**Kris Putnam-Walkerly,** philanthropy advisor and author of *Delusional Altruism*

"Whether you are a seasoned philanthropist or just finding your way, *Invitation to Impact* will encourage you to do more, give more, and make your community stronger for all. I highly recommend it."

—**Gloria Dittus,** chair, Story Partners

"*Invitation to Impact* provides a masterclass on transformational giving by harnessing the powers of the next-door humanitarians. As one of the hardest-working social impact leaders, Ms. Wendy Steele provides inspiring examples and meaningful guidance on how each of us can be champions and agents of change!"

—**Michelle Kim,** VP of Strategic Partnerships, TGR Foundation

"This book, just like its author, will inspire and motivate you to get involved, give back, and make an impact. As Wendy continues to demonstrate through her leadership, effective philanthropy is so much more than donating dollars. When you educate yourself to the needs and opportunities in a community and the people and organizations making lives better, those stories will open your heart to do more. This is a powerful read that reminds us that our past can shape our future and compassion can make a difference. If, like me, you're seeking a path to personal and community transformation, the stories and examples shared here can help light the way."

—**Debbie Ritchie,** managing director, Huron Group; founding president, Impact100 Pensacola Bay Area

INVITATION TO IMPACT

Lighting the Path to Community Transformation

WENDY H. STEELE

Published by MFF Publishing
Denver, CO
morgridgefamilyfoundation.org/publishing/
Copyright © 2023 Wendy H. Steele

All rights reserved.

Thank you for purchasing an authorized edition of this book and for complying with copyright law. No part of this book may be reproduced, stored in a retrieval system, or transmitted by any means, electronic, mechanical, photocopying, recording, or otherwise, without written permission from the copyright holder.

Distributed by River Grove Books

Design and composition by Greenleaf Book Group
Cover design by Liz Driesbach
Cover image © Shutterstock/benzeez

Publisher's Cataloging-in-Publication data is available.

Print ISBN: 979-8-9870082-0-1

eBook ISBN: 979-8-9870082-1-8

First Edition

For my family and friends, who forgive my long hours and travel, fill my life with boundless joy and love, and remind me every day what generosity looks like. I love you more than all the stars. You are remarkable.

For all the amazing women (and outstanding men) who join, support, and lead Impact100 chapters around the globe. You have exceeded my wildest expectations.

And for Gracie, who makes every video call a bit more human.

If you want to go fast, go alone. If you want to go far, go together.

—African Proverb

Contents

Foreword by Carrie Morgridge xiii
Preface: The World Needs Your Light xv

    Chapter 1: Not I, but We. 1
    Chapter 2: Community of Moms 9
    Chapter 3: Making Sense of the World 23
    Chapter 4: How Women Give. 33
    Chapter 5: What If? 49
    Chapter 6: Newsworthy 65
    Chapter 7: Transformation. 75
    Chapter 8: Million-Dollar Sunday. 83
    Chapter 9: Growing Pains 89
    Chapter 10: Global Movement 99
    Chapter 11: The Company You Keep. 111
    Chapter 12: When Disaster Strikes 123
    Chapter 13: Generosity Is Contagious 139
    Chapter 14: Building Trust. 155
    Chapter 15: Start Where You Are 171

Acknowledgments 175
Appendix 177
About the Author 185

Foreword

This book is about women's empowerment. It's about a movement: a collective giving model, built by a woman, for women, that democratizes giving.

At her absolute best, innovator and disrupter Wendy Steele will win your heart as she shares her strength and pain, openly and honestly. This book is about creating something big for women. It's about how all of us have something to give, and it's a guide on how to get started.

From an idea on the beach that launched a collective giving model, expanded nationally, then internationally, Wendy Steele's vision turned into a movement—a movement that you will want to be a part of.

This movement didn't just happen overnight. In fact, this idea was launched during one of our nation's hardest times, 9/11. Less than six months after the attack, Wendy fought back with a plan to change the giving world: Impact100!

Quietly and strongly, Impact100 has been growing in communities. Starting in Cincinnati, growing to more than sixty other United States cities, to Australia, and to the UK, this movement has given away over $100 million collectively—and they are just getting started!

INVITATION TO IMPACT

Wendy shares the design, growth, and some mistakes along the way as she invented Impact100. Read about some of the life-changing grants that were funded, or if you are ambitious like me, join a chapter—or all of them! There has never been a time like now when women have been so needed. We are needed for our brilliance, our ideas, and our ability to give back and change our communities. While most of us might not know a single woman who could write a $100,000 check, I bet most of us know a lot of women who could write a $1,000 check and collectively give $100,000.

We know that our trust in society has diminished. But did you know that giving circles are a way to combat that? Being involved with our own community, telling the truth, and leading are all ways that we can rebuild our society together.

Impact100 is a way for our voices to be heard. The last time I checked, $100 million is a really big deal, and together we can grow Impact100, help our communities, and not settle for the status quo.

—Carrie Morgridge
Co-founder, Morgridge Family Foundation

Preface

The World Needs Your Light

The year was 1923, and biologist Hugh Smith was deep in the mangrove forests of Thailand one night when, suddenly, the pitch darkness around him was illuminated for one magic moment. Stunned, Smith stopped moving and stared curiously into the darkness until the spectacle repeated itself.

As a scientist and professor, Smith searched for the most logical explanation for the phenomena. In time, he found the light originated from thousands of fireflies shining in unison. The truth was undeniable, and yet the underlying motivation for this dazzling showcase escaped scientists, mathematicians, and even biologists. Why would male fireflies all light up at the same time, if the goal of light signaling was for each to get his own mate? Haven't we all learned that competition is the behavioral paradigm that rules the natural world?

While it's true that competition may provide more drama for television and movies, it also would have driven humans extinct long ago had it been the only behavioral model for our species. Our survival and success depend on another natural strategy: cooperation. Time and time again, our species have been faced with challenges too great for any individual, from our ancestors coordinating for a hunt to the global COVID-19 vaccine effort. In these moments, our social capabilities allow us to work together and overcome insurmountable odds.

With respect to Professor Hugh Smith's discovery, scientists ultimately concluded that when the fireflies lit up together, their mating success rate skyrocketed from 3 percent to an astounding 82 percent.[1] Working as an interconnected community, a "positive system," was, in fact, exponentially more beneficial to the individuals and the whole community.

The concept embodied by these fireflies—that individuals working together to accomplish something extraordinary is not only a natural strategy, but a powerful one—is something I believe is also embodied by Impact100, the organization that began as a collective giving model I designed. It has since become a global giving movement with more than sixty-five chapters around the world, starting in 2001 in Cincinnati and now spanning from San Antonio, Texas, to Sydney, Australia.

More than twenty years on now, Impact100 has invited members from all walks of life to engage in meaningful giving while belonging to a supportive community of changemakers. Impact100 chapters identify and fund the local nonprofits that are solving the most pressing problems across our five broad Focus Areas: Arts & Culture, Education, Environment, Health & Wellness, and Family.

Looking at these individually, we can quickly see the value that each area brings to a local community. Arts and Culture includes both artistic and historical organizations of every kind that influence the very *cultural fiber* of a community.

The Education Focus Area is also very broad, encompassing traditional and nontraditional education nonprofits, as well as the many

---

1   John Bonner Buck, "Synchronous Rhythmic Flashing of Fireflies," *The Quarterly Review of Biology* 13, no. 3 (Fall 1938): 309–10.

circumstances that surround education, like transportation and anything that creates effective and healthy learning spaces.

The Environment Focus Area includes recreation and preservation of all ecosystems and organisms of the natural world.

Health and Wellness encompasses both mental and physical health, going beyond traditional medical interventions to include almost anything that can impact our well-being.

Finally, the most comprehensive Focus Area is our Family category, which relates to all actions and influences that contribute to supporting strong families.

When our Focus Areas are broadly interpreted, the mission of almost every nonprofit would qualify, and every woman in the community can find her passions and interests eligible for funding consideration. Only when all five of these areas are truly thriving can a community reach its highest potential.

By the end of 2022, Impact100 chapters around the globe had given away more than $123 million, and we are growing fast. Giving high-impact grants of $100,000 or more, most Impact100 chapters seek to reach at least five hundred members, who each donate $1,000 so they might lift every facet of their community by funding at least one grant in each of these areas.

Not only are the results of our giving visible and tangibly felt in communities around the world, but the impact of our giving model is also well-documented and backed by extensive research. I often say that Impact100 empowers women and transforms communities. In 2020, the Morgridge Family Foundation powered the first research study to determine whether these claims were true. The results exceeded my wildest expectations and validated what my instincts had led me to believe: Membership in Impact100 provides measurable increases in the primary characteristics of empowered people. Further, the research resoundingly supported the notion that communities are transformed by our significant grants. (More on this study can be found in chapter 14 and in the coffee table book *Impact100, Local Philanthropy Fueling a Global Movement* found at impact100global.org.)

According to best-selling author and speaker Shawn Achor, "Becoming a 'positive node' in your workplace, company, or community, and helping those around you improve their creativity, their productivity, their abilities, their performance, and more, you are not only helping the group become better; you are exponentially increasing your own potential for success."[2]

When we help others shine, that light reflects our own, making us brighter still and attracting more people to this important movement. For generations, society has taught us that we must compete to attain the highest goals. We are taught from an early age that being the best is how we become successful. We hear that success is a zero-sum endeavor—when there's a winner, there also has to be a loser—and is defined by our position at the top of the class. This false narrative states that our wins can only be attained by being smarter, stronger, or faster than our peers.

I started Impact100 because I knew the competition narrative was incomplete. I have always understood that despite popular culture's insistent messages to the contrary, we rise when we uplift others. Building and growing together is a more rewarding, enjoyable, and sustainable version of success than anything else we could accomplish alone. Today, Impact100 has given away more than $123 million in grants and engaged more than thirty thousand women and growing.

When I began Impact100, I never could have imagined the reach it would have today. I designed the model for women I had met in

---

[2] Shawn Achor, *Big Potential: How Transforming the Pursuit of Success Raises Our Achievement, Happiness, and Well-Being* (New York: Penguin Random House, 2018).

Cincinnati, and when additional women asked if I could help them do the same in their communities, I freely offered the structure of the Impact100 model along with all of the guidance and advice I could. The notion of empowering more women to give back in their local communities was exhilarating. Each new Impact100 chapter has been launched because someone hears about the model and commits to building one in their backyard. Impact100 chapters grow through the passionate belief of its members and their connections across communities, cultures, and vast geographies.

In 2015 I created Impact100 Global to provide better support to the women who launch new Impact100 chapters and lead existing chapters. Impact100 Global is the central connecting point, or node, facilitating broad sharing of Impact100 model best practices, technology, processes, and resources to Impact100 members across the globe. We know that once we begin collaborating and coordinating our best efforts, each of us shines a bit brighter—both as individuals and as a community. As we learn, share, and grow together, our collective and individual lights shine brighter, attracting others to join the movement—like fireflies.

At Impact100, we believe that too many women remain on the sidelines holding incredible light. We know well that today's problems are far too complex and urgent to be solved by only a few minds. Impact100 illuminates solutions by empowering women to come together in their local communities around the globe to identify and fund the solutions we need most. The Impact100 movement is a bright light in an increasingly dark world, empowering women to give, lead, and serve together.

We live in a connected world, where we rise and fall together. Let's choose to shine on together!

1

Not I, but We

What you do makes a difference, and you have to decide what kind of difference you want to make.

—Jane Goodall

When I was a child, my sisters and I would trick-or-treat for UNICEF each Halloween. Every October 31st, we would put on our little costumes we bought at the local store. Each had a stiff plastic face mask with a stretchy cord that kept it in place with round holes cut for our eyes and a thin oval slit for our mouths. Our costumes slipped over our heads like dresses and tied at the neck. Each year, we dressed up as superheroes or cartoon characters we liked from Saturday mornings in front of the TV. We would go from house to house, each of us carrying a small decorated box with a slot cut in the top. I remember the boxes had cartoon images of kids of different ethnicities holding hands, an illustration that each donation would equate to a carton of milk or a life-saving vaccination. Created by the United Nations Children's Fund to help kids in America fundraise for needy children around the globe, I remember feeling a sense of pride and accomplishment when I read the slogan "Kids Helping Kids" across the top.

So, when our neighbors answered our knock at the door, rather than holding up plastic pumpkins in hopes of receiving treats, we would explain that there were disadvantaged children in Africa who needed food and medical attention. In those days we always received a few coins or even small bills to support UNICEF. The nicest neighbors slipped us a candy bar or licorice as they smiled at our efforts to help children in faraway lands.

I don't remember what inspired us to start trick-or-treating for UNICEF, whether we were encouraged by our parents or a teacher from school. It was simply an idea we had one day—one that we acted on. But I don't recall any big conversations in which adults told us about the importance of giving back—what it meant to share our time, treasure, or talents with others. It was simply a part of who we were as a family.

We understood from our parents that each of us must do our best to leave the world better than we found it. Without much conversation, we picked up trash when we saw it, and helped our neighbors by shoveling snow or doing yard work. I vividly remember my dad telling us that since we were lucky enough to spend our summers in a beautiful place like Michigan, we should be up and out in the world no later than 9:00 a.m. each day. These small actions created the culture of our household, and in doing so my parents instilled in us a sense of gratitude and responsibility in our lives.

I was born in Connecticut, the middle daughter of three girls. My dad, a bright, funny, and engaging man, worked in Manhattan selling corrugated boxes to companies in the region. My beautiful, sensitive mom stayed home with us. When I was in elementary school, my dad was promoted at work, and we moved from Connecticut to St. Louis, Missouri, bringing him to the headquarters of his firm and expanding his responsibilities from regional to national. My parents made sure we understood that as members of the family, each of us should have age-appropriate responsibilities and contribute to the efficient running of the household.

Our chores would rotate but usually included doing our share of the tasks needed to sustain the house and family. Some happened daily, like washing the dishes, emptying the dishwasher, or feeding our dog, a Great Pyrenees named Pooh Bear. Some happened less frequently, like emptying the trash, raking leaves, or washing the patio furniture. As we grew up, our list of chores would expand commensurately. There was also yard work that included "scooping" the dog's waste from the yard, pulling weeds, and planting containers with annuals.

Although at the time I often felt we had more asked of us than many of our friends, I see in retrospect how useful developing this work ethic and sense of responsibility was in shaping who I am today. My sisters and I were raised with plenty of responsibility, chores, and strict rules to follow. For example, it was rare that we could go out several days in a row. I remember not being allowed to go to the skating rink or the mall with friends simply because I had gone over to a friend's house the day before. Earning the chance to go out with friends often included completing our homework and additional household chores. What at the time felt too strict actually provided benefits as I grew up.

This experience cultivated in me a deep appreciation for time with friends, which is something I still treasure and do not take for granted. My upbringing also reinforced the idea of doing the hard things first, a tactic I still use when scheduling my days. In an odd way, I think that having responsibilities and expectations from the adults in my life translated into confidence that I could complete the tasks well.

By the middle of eighth grade, most of my friends started talking about high school. Much to my surprise, many were leaving the local public school to attend a Catholic school in the area called St. Joseph's Academy. I had never heard of St. Joseph's Academy, but I knew I wanted to go there. I couldn't bear the thought of staying in public school without my best friends. I was able to convince my parents that this was a good idea, even if they were somewhat reluctant at first. Admission to St. Joe required passing a written entrance exam as well as getting through an interview with the head of school, Sister Mary DePaul. I was not the only one being interviewed—she also wanted to interview a parent. This would be complicated.

St. Joe was an all-girls Catholic high school, and our family was not Catholic. Although we were Christian, we were Protestant—and not regular churchgoers at that. My mom read the Bible sometimes and had the day-to-day faith that got you through the highs and lows of love and life. She described Jesus as a friend and told me how He loved the little children and called them to Him, but nothing she said was like the way my Catholic friends' parents spoke. My dad often said he "talked to God and felt His presence" on the water, in a boat, more clearly than when he was in a church. As for me, although I had a sense of who God was, I couldn't honestly say I'd read the Bible or could answer much about what was in it. Needless to say, I was nervous.

Sister Mary DePaul was a formidable woman with a stern demeanor and the kindest eyes. During the interview, we made small talk. I imagined she was trying to get to know me to assess whether I could join her school as a student. I was nervous and hoping not to say anything too stupid. Luckily, she didn't ask any questions about the Bible. Instead, we talked about the cute green plaid pleated skirts and crisp white shirts that comprise the foundation of the St. Joe uniform. At one point, she asked what I thought of the school motto, "Not I, but We," and I responded that it was sort of like "there's no 'I' in team," and we all need to work together to win. She seemed pleased and I was incredibly relieved. Perhaps I could be a St. Joe Angel after all.

When I received my acceptance letter, I was sure that Sister Mary DePaul had admitted me to St. Joseph's Academy as her pet project. I envisioned her worrying about me and trying to convince me to become a better Christian. To become a Catholic, maybe. I wasn't sure what her motive was; I was just grateful. Only years later would I understand that Sister Mary DePaul viewed every student as her "pet project" with a goal of helping them become their own unique people—who they were meant to become.

Summer comes to an end

August of 1977 marked the end of my last summer before starting high school. After another beautiful summer spent on Walloon Lake, Michigan, my family was preparing to head home to St. Louis. Leaving Michigan was always bittersweet. There, we enjoyed the freedom and fun of the summer; with unlimited time with our grandparents and so many fun things to do and see on the lake, it was tough to leave that all behind and go back to school. At the same time, I was ready to begin this new chapter in my life. I would soon be entering as a freshman at St. Joseph's Academy, and I was excited. I have always liked school and I especially looked forward to getting new brightly colored school supplies prior to the start of each new year.

INVITATION TO IMPACT

On the morning of August 7, Mom put the ingredients for our dinner in her crockpot and waved goodbye, promising to return in time for dinner that evening. Dad would be home from his business trip that afternoon and Grandma was expected for dinner. Mom headed out to go birdwatching and hike sand dunes about forty-five minutes from our cottage.

As an avid birdwatcher, Mom was most at home when she was out in nature. She could be hopeless navigating directions on roads and highways, but she never got lost in the woods. When she smiled, she lit up the room. She wore her heart on her sleeve, laughing and crying with equal ease. She was naive and trusting with a heart that was always open. Although Mom didn't believe in herself, she certainly believed in those around her.

That night, Dad arrived home as planned and so did Grandma, but Mom never made it back. It was the middle of the night before she was located. She had passed away on a sand dune. My sisters and I were told she was stung by a bee and had left her EpiPen too far away for her to reach the lifesaving antidote. We all knew about her allergy to yellowjackets. She was deathly allergic to wasps and had made the fatal mistake of not having her antidote with her. It had been a freak occurrence and she had passed away from the wasp's venom.

The twelve-hour drive home from Michigan that summer was particularly solemn. We were leaving our cottage, and, in the transition, our entire world shifted. Arriving home to St. Louis, the house felt strange. Everything looked just as it would have if Mom were still there. Her clothes, books, jewelry, and belongings were exactly as she'd left them, weeks before, when we drove away for our summer vacation. It was *weird*.

Even though everything looked the same, it felt completely different. I felt a sense of loss, of course, but mostly, I felt numb. Like a zombie in a movie, my life felt like it was in slow motion and I was just moving through the scenes, doing what had to be done. I purchased my school uniform and picked up school supplies as we sorted and donated much of Mom's clothing. The process was unimaginably difficult. I felt like I was walking through fog and mud, my progress so slow as to be almost invisible.

My enthusiasm for starting high school at St. Joseph's Academy seemed far away now. Although I had insisted that I attend this school so I could be with my friends, I couldn't escape feeling totally alone. As I arrived on my first day of school, the words "Not I, but We" seemed hollow. I couldn't see the "we." I could only feel the "I."

I was the only non-Catholic. I was the only one who didn't have a mom driving carpool. While my friends giggled or complained about what their moms packed in their lunch bags, I quietly ate the lunch I packed myself. I had no family in town, and my dad traveled frequently for work. Most days, I came home to an empty house. I didn't and couldn't see the "we" in my struggle or my loss. I felt so alone.

Sister Mary DePaul seemed to be everywhere at school. I saw her in the mornings as I headed into school and then again, many times throughout the day. She was always in the background, quietly observing. Something about her presence comforted me. Perhaps it was the way her kind eyes seemed to truly see me. Maybe it was the sweet smile that seemed to show genuine affection and amusement in all she observed. Without any overt gestures or big conversation, I knew her heart. She was a woman who could be relied upon if needed. She was steady and consistent.

It was then I knew that I was her project. Yes, along with every other student at St. Joe, I mattered to her, and she was working behind the scenes to encourage my success. I was starting to understand what our motto really meant.

2

Community of Moms

Alone we can do so little. Together we can do so much.

—Helen Keller

After Mom died, Dad hired our occasional babysitter, Mrs. Mitchell, on a weekly schedule. By this time, my older sister, Joanne, was off at boarding school, and only Tina, the youngest of the three of us, and I were still at home. Mrs. Mitchell had lost her only daughter after a long and painful battle with cancer. We connected deeply from a place of loss and of love. Three days a week, Mrs. Mitchell went grocery shopping before arriving in time to greet us after school. On these days, she made dinner for us and did some light housekeeping. When Dad traveled, Mrs. Mitchell stayed overnight.

She wasn't the only one who stepped in. I now seemed to have a community of moms. There were the moms who insisted on driving more carpool shifts because they were eager to get out of the house. There were the mom and daughter who invited me over after school. Whether baking chocolate chip cookies together or just doing homework, these afternoons gave a priceless sense of normalcy and of home.

These moms stayed with me throughout high school. They advised my dad on appropriate curfews and explained the difference between a private high school party and an open party. Still other moms stepped up in other ways to fill the void in my life and in our household. Sure, they delivered casseroles in the beginning. But their kindness didn't end there. They didn't leave in a week or a month or a semester. They stayed even when it was inconvenient.

The mom who took me shopping for my first formal dance will always hold a special place in my heart. Not only did she take me shopping, she also went the extra mile to help explain to my dad that, yes, this dress *was* modest and appropriate for a high school dance. She said that although the dress didn't come from Sears, it was a good value. I can still picture it, a long, straight dress in a subtle shade of blue.

At the hardest time in my young life, I benefited from the love and consideration of a community of moms. They came together organically and individually. No one made assignments and no one looked for praise or even acknowledgment. These moms just quietly did what they could, where they were, just because they saw a need and understood that a small act of kindness was worth the effort to a girl like me.

I finally understood the meaning of "Not I, but We." They had my back. They were there for me when it was convenient and remained long after. They didn't do it because they had to, or to gain recognition. No one truly knew how these women poured into my life. They did it because they saw a need before we could even articulate that we needed help. That's community.

Years later, in 2011, I read Bruce Feiler's book *The Council of Dads*, and it struck a familiar chord. Feiler describes that upon receiving a life-ending cancer diagnosis, he worried about his daughters going through life without him. He actively sought out six men who each knew him and understood different parts of his life in a uniquely personal way. Asking each to sign a pledge to share the life lessons they represented with the daughters he wouldn't be around to raise, Feiler created the Council of Dads. I now understood that growing up, even though I lost my mother at a young age, I had a "Council of Moms." I remain grateful for the gifts that come in times of loss and brokenness.

Grammy and Grampy

My maternal grandparents, Grammy and Grampy, also stepped up their support after Mom died. They spent their summers in Michigan, so we saw them frequently while we were up there too. During the school year, they lived in South Florida. I loved my time with them and admired them both.

Grampy spent his career as a banker and an entrepreneur. When I asked him what he was most proud of in his career, he said that during the Great Depression he had never once foreclosed on any of the bank's customers. Instead, he met with each farmer, father, and businessman (they were all men back then) in order to better understand their situation. He then created a modified repayment structure custom-tailored to each borrower and each unique circumstance. The goal was, of course, to repay the debt owed the bank, but to do it with the most manageable burden for the borrower. When he spoke, I could see his admiration and respect for each customer, even all those years later.

Savings accounts and investments were the same. Providing a return the family could not have achieved on their own allowed their nest eggs to grow. It was these accounts, these nest eggs, that would eventually fund a family's retirement. They would fund an education or a much-needed vacation for the family to visit faraway places. My grandfather beautifully described the important role that bankers played in the lives of all of their customers. I found it intriguing and hoped I could do something so significant in my career.

In this way, I came to see banking as a way to help people achieve more than they ever could on their own. A loan might enable a customer to start or grow a business. Mortgage loans allowed homeownership or education. Grampy explained that even saying no to a loan request was helpful. When I questioned this, he explained that he could calculate the likelihood of whether the customer could repay the debt according to its terms and based on their plans for the business. Declining a loan request saved the borrower from taking on too much debt. It also encouraged them to revisit their business plan, reconsider their needs, and often resubmit a more reasonable request to the bank.

When I visited Grammy and Grampy, I spent most of my time with Grammy. Together, we shopped, had lunch, walked the beach, and swam in both the Gulf of Mexico and their backyard pool. Grammy taught me all about the shells on the beach. She had a great collection she had picked up over the years. They were displayed beautifully throughout their home. We would walk for miles together, shelling and watching for dolphins.

Grammy was tall and lovely with impeccable manners and a beautiful way with words. She played bridge and golf and was excellent at needlepoint. More than her looks or hobbies or how she carried herself, what people noticed most about Grammy was how she made you feel. She was an excellent hostess. No matter how big the group or who was assembled, Grammy made each person feel special. She had a way of making conversation that encouraged the other people to speak while validating all they shared with her. She asked the sort of questions in conversations that prompted an authentic and unrehearsed response. Grammy had the uncanny ability to make each person with her, whether in a big crowd or alone, feel they belonged.

Honored Guest Program

It was Grammy who designed the Honored Guest Program, where each grandchild was invited, one at a time, to visit with them for several days in Florida.

Visiting Grammy and Grampy was incredibly special. They had a red felt runner with gold glitter spelling out "red carpet" with a scripted flourish. When we arrived home from the airport, Grammy insisted I enter first and walk on the red carpet, since it was rolled out just for me. Every meal was a combination of my favorite foods, and each activity was orchestrated to my tastes and interests.

For me, this meant plenty of time on the beach and spending as much time as possible with Grammy and Grampy. I adored them both more than I could ever describe. My visits developed a familiar rhythm: I joined Grammy and Grampy for breakfast each morning. Grampy, I understood, was a morning person. He loved to get up early and go to bed early. Grammy, on the other hand, was decidedly a night owl. Mornings were not her friend, so she was often quiet around the breakfast table. But she was always there, and although she wasn't very chatty in the mornings, she always wore a smile.

Grampy would eat his breakfast while reading the morning papers. He subscribed to several and always made a point of reading each one cover to cover. He was actually allergic to the ink on the newsprint, so each morning, the newspapers were placed in the warming drawer of the oven to dry out until he was ready to read them. Despite this, Grampy typically sniffled his way through most of breakfast. This reaction did not deaden his sense of humor or diminish his interest in reading the news. He often shared his favorite comic strip or news story of the day with Grammy and me. *Hägar the Horrible* was always doing something hilarious, prompting Grampy to erupt in laughter as he tried to explain the humor, before thrusting the paper in our direction so we could read it for ourselves and join in the laughter.

Lessons learned walking the beach

A quick review of the tide tables would dictate when Grammy and I took our beach walk together. We walked at least once every day, but the timing was critical. I learned early on from Grammy that walking at low tide was the best time to walk, so long as it wasn't too early in the morning.

Low tide exposed hard-packed sand, which made our walks easier. More importantly, low tide was best for shelling, as the receding water revealed so many treasures otherwise concealed by the rush of waves. If absolutely necessary, we sometimes had to compromise and take our walk during a middle-low tide. The sand was still hard-packed for better traction and at least some shells were exposed for keen-eyed shellers. We would never walk at high tide, however. The soft sand was far too difficult to walk on and everyone knew there were no good shells to be found at high tide.

Each time we headed off for a walk, Grammy did a quick assessment of the wind direction and strength. If we were planning a particularly long walk, she would look ahead at the forecast as well. Rather than decide our walking route based on how crowded the beach looked or where we had found success shelling the day before, the wind directed our steps. Grammy used the wind to determine whether we walked to the left or to the right once our feet hit the sand.

Always best, she advised, was to begin our walk facing into the wind. At the start of our walk, she reasoned, we had more energy and were eager to get going, so a bit of a headwind wouldn't slow us down. The payoff would come on the return home. With the wind at our backs, we reaped the benefits of this extra propulsion when we needed it most: at the end of our walk, when we were tired and—hopefully—laden with shells or other beach treasures we'd collected on our journey together.

We typically walked side by side along the water's edge or the so-called shell line, chatting and showing each other our finds. Along the way we had to navigate several groins—long, narrow structures designed to prevent beach erosion on the beach path. Groins can take many forms, but the ones we passed most often resembled eight- to ten-foot-tall pieces of lumber planted from the sand out to the water in a tight pattern.

When passing through a groin, we always went single file, one behind the other. Grammy told me about an old mariner's tale that said different paths through the groin would foretell an argument later between people who chose different paths. Couples who consistently chose different paths were destined for marital problems. Although I wouldn't say my grandmother was generally superstitious, this practice was one that mattered to her. If I inadvertently went through a different group of pillars, she would stop and quietly wait for me to double back and come through again—this time, in her footsteps. If my grandfather was walking with us, she let him lead and we would both follow his footsteps.

Grammy was quite knowledgeable about shells. She taught me the names and shared other facts about them and how they grew. She was discerning about what she picked up and brought home. As a young girl, I was happy to find any unbroken shell, and often had a sack full of similar shells. But Grammy was selective, only bringing home a shell that would enhance her collection in some way with its unique color or shape. I loved learning anything from Grammy, but our beach walks brought so much opportunity to expand my knowledge of the beach and its inhabitants. Some of the shell names were easy to remember because they were so descriptive.

For example, I often collected baby's cradle (which was also called a slipper shell), cat's paw, turkey wing, and shark eye shells on our walks. With practice, I got more and more skilled at finding and identifying shells along the shore. As my skills and experience expanded, so did my discernment. It wasn't long before my favorite shells were the ones that were less plentiful. By my late teens and early twenties, I considered it a true prize to find a lightning whelk, tulip shell, sand dollar, murex, or conch shell of any variety. Even today, seeing certain shells takes me right back to my childhood walks with her.

When looking for shells, Grammy always reminded me not to forget to lift my gaze and look for the horizon in the Gulf of Mexico. There was so much to see and hear and even smell when we walked the beach together. I learned that only when we lift our eyes do we see those unexpected miracles in our midst. By looking up, we'd catch a glimpse of a graceful dolphin breaking out of the waves and splashing back in, a stingray fluttering close to shore, or a beautiful boat on the horizon with its sails filled with wind.

This lesson echoed in my mind many years later, while volunteering with several nonprofit organizations. The arduous and often monotonous task of fundraising kept many leaders' heads down, focused on those important details. As a result, they often missed aiming for bigger goals and more strategic planning. This condition is what informed the Impact100 model of significant grants of $100,000 or more. With funding like that, our nonprofit applicants are invited to dream big and imagine what a grant like that could do for their organization and the community it serves.

Grammy taught me not to let the task at hand become so all-consuming it was detrimental. Sometimes when I walked the beach looking for shells, I found myself in intense concentration watching my feet. Although it's important to avoid stepping on something sharp or missing a beautiful shell, Grammy taught me that there is a balance between keeping your eye on the project at hand and lifting your eyes to see the world around you. We shouldn't get so caught up in the task that we miss the beauty all around us.

Grammy worried that our habit of beach-walking and shelling would result in poor posture for me, an occupational hazard that some avid shellers call "sheller's stoop," which was to be avoided at all costs. As I walked the beach in such deep concentration that my head was down and my shoulders rounded, she would gently place her index finger between my shoulder blades as a reminder to straighten up. Grammy explained that good posture was closely correlated with good bone and muscle health, so she was diligent in reminding me to straighten up when my shoulders slumped and my neck angled down toward the sand. In today's world when we all have our bodies huddled around our cell phones and tablets, I can sometimes feel her gentle touch between my shoulder blades, reminding me to straighten up.

We typically reconnected with Grampy for cocktail hour and to watch the sunset, hoping to see the green flash. Once the sun dipped into the Gulf, it was our signal to take our seats in the dining room to enjoy dinner together. We shared delicious food and comfortable conversation as we exchanged stories of our adventures that day.

Conversation always flowed comfortably with my mother's parents. Grampy was a great storyteller, so he would often share embellished stories from his youth or share with great enthusiasm about his winning golf shot or fun meeting that day. No subject was off-limits. They often asked me all kinds of questions—about my studies, my friends, and my school activities—and they paid attention as I answered. They gave advice but didn't lecture. They asked questions so they truly understood my viewpoint on the subject at hand. I loved every minute with them. We talked news, politics, current books or movies, and values. Neither of them ever monopolized the conversation. They were not trying to instill their views of the world, but rather they were hoping to instill in me a way to think about the world. I only wish more people approached conversations and tightly held opinions with the same spirit today.

Jigsaw puzzles

After dinner, Grampy retreated to the den to read the evening paper and watch a bit of TV before going to bed early. Grammy and I selected a jigsaw puzzle from her large collection and spent every evening, and the occasional rainy day, working to complete it.

Grammy was an expert puzzler. After emptying the box of its contents and carefully arranging each piece face-up on the table, we put the box out of sight on the floor below us. With a floor lamp pulled close by, we sat together piecing together the colorful image. We did the edges first, and after that, we each selected a color or pattern we were collecting in hopes of building a section of the puzzle.

Without the benefit of having the full puzzle displayed on the box top, each puzzle piece became more challenging.

I treasured these evenings. We were creating something beautiful together, often surprising ourselves with the design as we progressed. Our conversation was relaxed as we focused on the task together of reaching this common goal. We would only abandon the puzzle for the evening when we were too tired to work anymore. Unless it was my last night, then we stayed up until it was finished, sometimes well past my bedtime.

Finding my new role in the family

A lot of things changed when my mother died, but not as much as you might expect. You see, my mom was a recovering alcoholic who struggled with depression and low self-esteem. She was well for periods of time, but then her illness would creep back in, and she'd stay confined in her darkened bedroom with migraine headaches that seemed to last for days.

One of the biggest changes that happened for me was that, after Mom died, I began attending my younger sister Tina's parent-teacher conferences, helping her with homework, and taking on extra chores around the house. Most of all, I worked hard in school and tried to help my dad as much as possible. I hung out with Dad and watched TV with him when he got home at night. That's when we would talk through how Tina was doing in school, any upcoming events, as well as Dad's travel plans.

My sister Joanne is three years older and enjoyed her status as the eldest. Early on, she established herself as the "rebel." Any door she came across that said "Do not enter," Joanne flung open and sashayed through. She was strong-willed and a bit stubborn. Always up for an adventure or new experience, she pushed limits and boldly made her way in the world. Eager to grow up and be independent, when Joanne was offered an opportunity to attend a boarding school in the Berkshires of Massachusetts, she jumped at the chance. Joanne saw it as an opportunity to experience the freedom and benefits of college while still in high school, and she was elated to leave home and launch into the first steps of adulthood.

My sister Tina, who is four years my junior and seven years younger than Joanne, was always petite and a bit shy. As the baby of the family, she was doted upon and well-loved. Growing up, she was playful and loved to be outside. She could entertain herself for hours searching for bugs or digging in the mud. Once, while the family was on vacation, a butterfly landed on Tina's shoulder and stayed there for hours. With patience well beyond her years, Tina held still or moved very slowly so as not to startle the winged beauty from its perch.

As for me, I became the peacemaker and rule-follower. I've always been quick to help and eager to do the right thing. I remember, at about twelve or thirteen years old, making a conscious decision to stay out of trouble in order to help my parents and reduce the stress in our household. I was the helper and encourager, trying not to make waves or disappoint.

Growing up this way allowed my "empathy muscle"—as I like to think of it—to really develop. I paid keen attention to the needs of those around me, especially in my family, but this also transitioned well to school or work environments. In every situation, whether at school or at home, I determined what success looked like, or what was needed, and then I sought to deliver it. While Joanne was off at school, anticipating what Dad or Tina would need and quietly doing whatever that was became my habit.

From my hands-on experience, growing up this way, I learned to define empathy as putting myself in someone else's place and understanding what they are going through. Compassion takes the understanding gained from empathy and adds action. Feeling (empathy) without action (compassion) can be draining: You ache for others but do not work to help them. When I feel empathy and then act, I not only improve the situation for the target of my compassion, but I also feel as if I have made a difference, which makes me feel better.

I often describe empathy and compassion as muscles. Although I believe we can be naturally empathetic and compassionate, intentionally working those skills makes us better at them.

3

Making Sense of the World

> It seems like the more I give the more I get, and
> that is the way it is supposed to go in life.
>
> —Dolly Parton

My four years at St. Joe flew by. At the same time, as I lined up with my classmates in our white caps and gowns on our graduation day, I was a very different girl than the one who'd walked into St. Joseph's Academy four years earlier as a freshman. This place and these people had become part of my extended family. They had certainly been there for me and my whole family over the years. I was filled with gratitude.

At eighteen years of age, my faith was new and sort of simple. My vision of God was of a fair and just Father figure who sat in a raised chair, allotting good and bad times in equal measure to each of us. I was sure that because I had already endured some really deep waters by the time I graduated high school, the rest of my life would be easy. I was so relieved!

I actually felt bad for some of my classmates. Those girls in high school who just seemed to live a charmed life with great parents, great grades, great college prospects, and not a worry in the world? I was afraid they would be blindsided and completely unprepared to handle difficult times when it was their turn. I worried about how they would fare with so little preparation. I actually felt grateful that I had gotten the hard stuff over with before graduating high school. I am not sure where I came to that conclusion, but it brought me great comfort back then.

Learning another hard truth

The origin of my naive relief at having "gotten the hard stuff over with" was not the only truth that eluded me. I hadn't yet learned the truth about my mother's death. But that summer after high school graduation, I learned that the story of Mom having died from an insect sting was not true.

The truth was she had taken her own life. She struggled with depression and never truly felt she had value in the world. With only a vague understanding of mental illness, I was crushed by learning the truth that she *chose* to leave us. She sought out the most peaceful place she knew and had even taken the time to write us a brief note. Hearing all this made me feel like I was losing her all over again. Learning this new truth pierced my belief that my troubles were all behind me. Reflecting on this newfound truth all these years later, what comes to mind is years of never talking about my mom—never recognizing her birthday, date of death, or anything to do with who she was in life. It was as if the way she died was so incredibly painful for all of the family, it erased or "broke" the natural desire to remember her in any way beyond the mental illness that ended her life.

Thankfully, people are better now at understanding like my mom's, but then, it was considered taboo to like suicide, addiction, and mental illness.

Yet all these years later, I remain grateful for the difficult times in my life. We learn a lot when we achieve success, but enduring through life's greatest challenges is how we grow. The real lessons come in the valleys. In desert places, we gain important perspectives, stretch ourselves in new ways, and learn or strengthen our resilience. It is where we learn the truth of who we are. We test and deepen friendships; we deepen our faith and learn skills we never knew we would need. Our values become amplified and simplified when times are hard.

Connecticut College

Arriving at Connecticut College as a freshman, I was nervous and excited in equal measure. From the minute I first stepped on campus while touring potential schools with my dad, this place felt special. It felt right. Arriving that first day, however, I knew very well that this day almost hadn't happened.

When my classmates and I were still juniors in high school, the halls of St. Joe had been buzzing with talk of college. We'd each had dreams and expectations about what college would be like and where we would go. Most of my classmates planned to stay fairly close to home. The in-state colleges and universities were strong and attractive. If leaving Missouri, popular options were most often faith-based, Southern, or both, including schools such as St. Mary's at Notre Dame, Vanderbilt, Texas Christian University, and Ole Miss.

When it came to college selection, my dad had opinions that were in stark contrast to most of my friends' families. He encouraged me to attend a school in another part of the country. That way, in addition to whatever I studied in school, I would also learn about a region of the country I might want to live in at some point. Since he and his brother had graduated from Harvard, he insisted we explore the East Coast schools first.

The two of us planned a trip to tour several schools from Connecticut to New Hampshire. This was a fun trip for me and the first time I had ever traveled with Dad by myself. It was exciting. We talked through several potential schools as we went from campus to campus. Although he would have loved to have me attend Harvard, it never felt like the right place for me. In fact, no campus truly stood out for me until we visited Connecticut College.

Seeing the campus for the first time took my breath away. The place was so beautiful. My graduating class would be relatively small, yet at more than four hundred students, big enough to always be meeting new people. Connecticut College was my clear first choice. But I was far from a shoo-in. I was, in fact, the first person in the history of St. Joseph's Academy to ever apply to the school. Although my grades were good, Jeanette Hersey, the dean of admissions, had no understanding of the academic rigor of my high school.

Ultimately, I was wait-listed at Connecticut College. With no assurance that my status would be converted to an acceptance, I resigned myself to attending the school that was a distant second to Connecticut College, with hopes of transferring in my sophomore year. Much to my surprise and delight, about three weeks before I was to leave for college, a phone call came to change the course of my life. I was accepted! Dean Hersey explained when she called that they were sure a dorm would become available for me, but I would have to reside in temporary housing until a proper dorm room opened up. That was fine with me. I was just so happy to be accepted to the school I was sure would be the ideal place for me. The housing could be sorted out later.

After moving far away from home, family, and friends and living in temporary housing (in the infirmary), I found myself questioning my decision. Connecticut College no longer seemed like my dream school. Instead, I felt like a fish out of water and was overwhelmed with feelings of isolation and loneliness. Tearful calls home to my dad were met with advice to be patient, to give Connecticut College and the college community more of a chance. He was sure everything would be better when I moved into my dorm. I remained hopeful but miserable, mad at myself for making such a stupid choice.

Through my tears and my doubts, I decided to stay the course. Partly, I suppose, because I couldn't let go of the feeling that I was where I was supposed to be, and partly because I couldn't imagine "quitting" so quickly and giving up my dream of college life at Conn. The campus was so incredibly beautiful, with old stone buildings, gorgeous lawns, and sweeping views of the Thames River and Long Island Sound. There was a darling chapel with a friendly priest who made me feel welcome; professors and students were friendly and helpful. Perhaps here I would find the kind of community I had grown to rely upon. These glimmers of hope reminded me that often, things can be hard in the beginning, but the hard times make room for wonderful things to follow.

I was only in the infirmary's temporary housing a few weeks before dorm space opened up. I was assigned a single room (no roommate!) on the first floor of a dorm called Windham. Things were looking up, or so I hoped. Moving in, I discovered a stark reality of college life in contrast to my high school experience—boys and girls lived next door to each other and shared co-ed bathrooms on the floor. Yikes.

This naive girl from a family of sisters and an all-girls Catholic school in the Midwest was in culture shock.

Things began to turn around when I met a wonderful girl from New York and a girl from Wilmington, Delaware, who would become my closest friends. Soon after I moved in, some boys kicking a soccer ball in the hall saw the sailing photos on my wall and asked if I could sail. They were on the team and needed a crew. I jumped at the chance. Not long after getting settled into Windham, the tears dried up and Connecticut College became all I had hoped it would.

Over the next four years, I would laugh and cry and dance and learn more than I could have hoped. I met amazing people and made great friends. I thrived on the sailing team, crewing for an excellent sailor and alongside a high-performing group of sailors and friends.

As an economics major, I hoped to follow in my grandfather's footsteps and become a banker. When I graduated in 1985, private banking was a new field, and I loved the concept. I entered the banking business in order to help people. I wanted to serve, and I was sure this was a great way to do just that.

Finding my purpose

After graduation, I entered a nine-month training program at a regional bank in Hartford, Connecticut, to learn the skills needed to serve high-net-worth families in every capacity the bank offered. I thrived in my banking career, got married, and lived and worked in several Connecticut communities, including Farmington, Greenwich, and New Haven, as well as spending several years in Boston, Massachusetts.

My husband and I settled in New Haven, Connecticut, in 1990 and thought it might be time to start a family. Preparing for a new addition and anticipating the need for a nanny, we renovated our home to include a separate living space for the presumed caregiver, and I negotiated a four-day workweek with an additional provision allowing me to work from home one day each week. I am a planner by nature, and this was a well-planned transition from married couple to family in New England.

Perhaps you've heard the Yiddish expression "Man plans, and God laughs." Well, let's just say things didn't quite go according to plan. About six months before my due date, my husband received an offer to join a Midwest regional bank headquartered in Cincinnati, Ohio, and he really wanted to accept the position. It was a great opportunity for him, and given the cost of living in Cincinnati, I would be able to choose whether—and how much—I wanted to work after the baby came. It seemed like a great opportunity, so in 1992, we adjusted our plans and moved to Cincinnati.

Cincinnati is a great place to live. The people are friendly and welcoming. The city is also geographically beautiful—built on seven beautiful hills that roll and rise, creating a lovely, ever-changing landscape. In addition, the cost of living in Cincinnati is relatively low, much lower than any East Coast city I have lived in, yet there are so many corporate headquarters in the area and well-paying jobs. In this way, the city reminds me a bit of St. Louis, where I grew up. I remember my dad used to talk about the great economic benefits of living there. These are places where the math works in your favor; high-paying jobs and a low cost of living is like winning the lottery.

I moved to Cincinnati not knowing a soul, but that didn't last long. I met so many great people and made lifelong friendships. These were people in my neighborhood, people I worked with, and people I met through community service. I've found that the best way to get to know a community is to connect through service. I volunteered at our church, at preschool, and at local nonprofits. The Junior

League membership I had in Connecticut allowed me to transfer to Cincinnati's League, where I met more amazing and dynamic women. Cincinnati has a vibrant nonprofit community, and I enjoyed learning about the solutions provided by dedicated people around the area. I also learned about the tremendous needs our most vulnerable neighbors faced.

I've always been a generalist in my approach to community service. I don't have a single passion, such as feeding the hungry or rescuing animals. I have a deep passion for the people and organizations who have found the best solutions to the problems they are most connected to. Those are the nonprofits I support and the people I admire. I believe that vibrant communities need a full spectrum of opportunities, services, and solutions in order to truly thrive. With this in mind, I had the good fortune to volunteer, donate, and serve on boards of nonprofits that are solving a wide variety of problems.

I learned so much from my involvement. I learned about issues facing my neighbors and the solutions offered by local nonprofits who worked tirelessly to bring relief. I also heard their stories of applying for grants, constantly in search of funding. The donations they received were awesome, and they were thankful. But often these gifts served as Band-Aids that merely got them through that cycle, that day, or that crisis. Tomorrow they would need to be back out, seeking, asking, and sharing their vision of what could be possible for our community. Their mission was exhausting, but it was important, so they pressed on, telling their stories, sharing their vision, and asking for support.

Over the years, as I got involved in different organizations and projects, I would excitedly share the work of a particular organization and invite my friends to join me in this cause. I was surprised to hear all the varied but legitimate reasons they felt they couldn't join me. Sometimes the cause or subject matter didn't align with their priorities. For example, I was involved in a health and human service organization, and the woman I invited to help was only passionate about improving the arts and culture scene in our community.

More often the issue was time. For example, a stay-at-home mom would tell me she couldn't afford to pay a sitter to watch her kids for ten dollars an hour while she volunteered with me. Friends who worked outside the home full-time explained that they couldn't take time off to join me. I also heard from women who traveled for work and would have to miss the regular meetings.

When asked to give, women also wondered aloud where the money went and when it would be spent. They said when they had given in the past, they never really knew what happened to their donation. Did it even make a difference? Did their donation matter at all to the causes they cared about? They doubted it had made any dent in the problem they were hoping to solve. They shared a story they'd heard about a nonprofit CEO who made a seven-figure salary and flew on his own private plane and concluded "they are all like that—it's a racket."

Most troubling was the notion that what they had wasn't *enough*—they didn't have enough money, time, or talent to make a real difference in the weighty problems they saw around them.

Having it all: the evolution of a working mom

I loved my career and I loved being a mom. My first child, Stephen, was born shortly after my husband's career took us to Cincinnati. Although I had received job offers, I was uncertain about how the end of my pregnancy would go and I had no idea how committed to my career I would feel once Stephen was "on the outside," as we used to joke. I declined the offers, in part because they never felt like the "right" position at the "right" firm, and in part because I wanted to keep my options open to create the role that best complemented my new role as Mom.

As women, we endlessly debate, discuss, and struggle to find that elusive thing called "balance." Or, the way popular culture often describes it, we search for the path that leads to "having it all." In the struggle to find the ideal, sometimes we forget that our definition of ideal is as fluid as our growing families, our priorities, and our life circumstances. At least that has been true for me.

A few months before Stephen's second birthday, his brother, Alex, came along, and then a few months after Alex's second birthday, Hailey was born. Needless to say, my definitions of success, family, and balance shifted quite a bit in those years. During these early years, as the family grew and changed, my role morphed, along with the family dynamics. Illustrating that there is not a one-size-fits-all way to manage a growing family and a career, I enjoyed my time over the years as a full-time, stay-at-home mom, and later worked from home for a company in another state (making me an early adopter of remote work!). At some points I also worked part-time, and later I was employed full-time outside the home. I had the great benefit of finding amazing childcare and having understanding clients and leaders at work. My situation wasn't perfect, but it worked. Most of the time.

4

How Women Give

If you want to see things happen at a global level, start at the village level. Give women the tools and education and they will drive the change.

—Melinda Gates

When I was in my early thirties, I heard a story about a church in financial difficulty. It wasn't a local church, but it stuck with me. Something unexpected had happened to disrupt the church's finances, so the senior pastor called together the head of the men's group, Jerome, and the head of the women's group, Kelly, to discuss the situation.

In order to meet their financial obligations, the church needed to raise a lot of money and do it quickly. Kelly rushed off after the meeting and gathered her team. Over the next few weeks, the women's group held bake sales, rummage sales, and car washes. By the time she returned to the pastor's office three weeks later, Kelly was exhausted yet delighted to deliver a check for more than $8,000!

She had never raised this much money in her life, and it was thrilling to know she would be a part of the solution to her church's financial crisis.

As Kelly was walking out of the pastor's office, Jerome was just arriving. She stuck around to hear his news. What she heard was surprising. Jerome handed the pastor a check for many times more than she had just delivered. She was floored to see this and couldn't understand how in the world he'd accomplished this feat. She knew he and his family had been out of town for part of the time and that his company was amid its busy season.

When asked how he'd raised that much money so quickly, Jerome replied that he'd reviewed his own finances and decided how much his family could personally give, and with that number in mind, he'd reached out to several of his male friends involved at the church. He not only shared what he and his family were willing to give, but also asked them to dig deep and consider their financial contribution. He was delighted by the generosity of the men in his life and the fact that they could all quickly rally to the aid of the church.

Kelly was shocked! It never even occurred to her to write a check, or to ask her women friends to do the same. Now, that is not because men kept her from writing a check. It was simply that check writing was not a solution that came to mind quickly for her or the other women in her community. She imagined how much more productive they might have been had they done a combination of service-based fundraising along with simple, powerful check writing.

This story was a powerful lesson for me, and it can be for you too. At a societal level, women need to be reminded there are many ways we can give back—and volunteering our time and talent is only the beginning. We can also choose to provide financial support to the causes we care about.

As a former banker, I know that it wasn't until the Equal Credit Opportunity Act of 1974 that women were able to get separate credit cards from their husbands. And as late as 1988, the Women's Business Ownership Act was passed, allowing women to obtain a business loan without a male co-signer. Women's financial freedom was still a relatively new concept, and consequently, women didn't have the same financial relationship to their philanthropic giving as men did. Women have been conditioned to think that their contributions are best made in the form of bake sales and volunteer hours. By 2001, I personally knew that mindset was outdated, and I wanted to share that realization with other women. I wanted women to give in whatever style best suited them—including writing a check.

Historically, giving is gendered

Today, I am often asked why Impact100 is exclusively a women's organization in the United States. (In Australia, Impact100 includes both men and women.) The answer is rooted in the cultural context of American women's financial autonomy, post-1974. These days, women in the United States are certainly financially capable and legally able to be philanthropic donors, but in practice, there seems to be a barrier stopping us from doing so. I know women are givers and care deeply about their local communities, and that they are reaching financial independence and breaking through glass ceilings in nearly every profession.

So, what's the issue? Well, while American women's financial prospects may finally be approaching equal to those of men, there are well-documented differences in the way men and women give. Take the findings of several 2015 studies by the Indiana University Lilly Family School of Philanthropy. One study found that, for starters, women are more likely to give and to give in higher amounts than their male counterparts.[3] Moreover, women are more likely to volunteer their time—33 percent, compared to 26–29 percent of men—and volunteer more time than men.[4]

The gender differences in giving begin with motivation. Studies have found that empathy works as a significant motivator for women but not for men. Instead, men say they give from a strategic mindset that considers the tax benefits of giving, and women feel less confident about tax strategies and investment options related to their philanthropy.[5] For women, giving is an experience they want to be connected to, so they can see and create a positive change in the world.

For women, successful giving engages both the head and heart. Perhaps that is why women are more likely to participate in collaborative giving and giving circles; 81 percent of giving circles (like Impact100) are majority-women groups, and more than 50 percent are women-only groups[6]—and giving circles have contributed up to $1.29 billion to philanthropy since their inception. These networks can offer the educational, social, and emotional pillars that support a holistic approach to giving. Additionally, women are more likely to give to organizations where they can see the impact of their giving,

---

3   Debra Mesch, Una Osili, Jacqueline Ackerman, and Elizabeth Dale, "Do Women Give More?: Findings from Three Unique Data Sets on Charitable Giving," IUPUI Women's Philanthropy Institute, Lilly Family School of Philanthropy, September 2015, 12–15, https://scholarworks.iupui.edu/handle/1805/6984.
4   Debra Mesch, Una Osili, Jacqueline Ackerman, and Elizabeth Dale, "How and Why Women Give: Current and Future Directions for Research on Women's Philanthropy," IUPUI Women's Philanthropy Institute, Lilly Family School of Philanthropy, May 2015, 33, https://hdl.handle.net/1805/6983.
5   Mesch et al., "How and Why Women Give," 13–17.
6   Mesch et al., "How and Why Women Give," 36.

and on average they want to be involved with organizations to which they donate money.[7]

One industry study of high-net-worth households found that women were more likely than men to say that impact is an important factor in their investment decisions. In this same study, women were also more likely than men to say:

- They feel investment decisions are a way they express their values.
- They prefer to invest in companies with a positive social or environmental impact; they avoid investing in companies with harmful impacts and review their portfolios with this in mind.
- They make investment decisions that support issues important to them.
- They see impact investing as the "right thing to do as a responsible citizen and investor."[8]

Spiral notebook

After school let out in the summer of 2001, I packed up the kids and our golden retriever, Shadow, and headed to Northern Michigan to relax and spend time with my dad and stepmom, Cynny. At

---

[7] Collective Giving Research Group, "Giving Circle Membership: How Collective Giving Impacts Donors," Collective Giving Research Group, November 2018, https://scholarworks.iupui.edu/bitstream/handle/1805/17743/giving-circle-membership18.pdf?sequence=1&isAllowed=y.

[8] Anna Zakrzewski, Kedra Newsom Reeves, Michael Kahlich, Maximilian Klein, Andrea Real Mattar, and Stephan Knobel, "Managing the Next Decade of Women's Wealth," Boston Consulting Group, April 9, 2020, https://www.bcg.com/publications/2020/managing-next-decade-women-wealth.

thirty-eight, my life was full, and I needed a break from the pace of full-time work as a private banker, mother of three, and general household manager. Escaping the heat and humidity of Cincinnati summers and, instead, basking in the cool nights and warm days on the lakeshore seemed a perfect way to unplug and reconnect to my parents and my children. Summer "up north" typically included jigsaw puzzles, campfires, and lots of family time. This particular summer escape delivered on all fronts.

Despite the slower pace and intentional disconnection from work life—or perhaps because of it—I kept thinking about the women back home in Cincinnati. I ruminated about the nonprofits doing so much to make our community stronger, better, and more resilient. I simply couldn't get these thoughts off my mind. I did what I often do: I tried to put it all on paper and sort out my thoughts.

Pulling a spiral notebook from my bag, I began to write down every objection to giving I'd heard from my women friends in Cincinnati. Their barriers to community service were real. There were so many reasons—*legitimate* reasons—why women were not involved in their community. I felt these barriers were keeping women from participating in their own communities in a meaningful way. I realized that although women's roles had changed and evolved over several generations, our philanthropy had not kept up. I knew that the community needed these women. It needed their hearts, their brains, and their checkbooks. These women needed to know what it felt like to be a part of the solution. They needed a viable path to community service and philanthropy that matched their current, ever-changing lives.

First and foremost, I needed to redesign how women contributed to making their community a better place to live. Historically, women gave their time. But in today's world, time was often the most precious commodity that we couldn't always give away. Women needed a path to unleash the potential they *could* afford to give. We were not the one-size-fits-all community of women portrayed by traditional philanthropy. In fact, had we ever been?

We needed flexibility. Our lives seemed to run in seasons. There were times when we had plenty of time to give and would relish hands-on community engagement. During other seasons, we were so time constrained, it was hard to imagine adding anything to our already packed days. The idea was to allow women the opportunity to design their own involvement. Should they choose to get involved, they needed an experience that could provide a robust way for them to learn, grow, connect, and make a difference.

For example, a woman might choose to become deeply engaged in the grant review process for the funding focus area she was most interested in. She would be trained on how to properly vet an application, make a site visit, and assess a nonprofit's plans to spend a potential grant award. When life changes and an aging parent needs help, a child gets engaged or has a baby, or any one of hundreds of other important reasons pop up to pull the woman away from volunteering, she can seamlessly shift her attention to the home front without repercussion or guilty feelings.

Further, if women chose not to be involved, they wouldn't be penalized, criticized, or made to feel guilty by their choices. In addition, the decision shouldn't have to be a permanent one. Life is full of unexpected events that influence our ability to give of our time. Women needed to be able to pivot easily and quickly when needed.

Being a private banker, I like numbers that make sense. I like big, meaningful, round numbers. What if women were asked to give $1,000? That's significant; that's an amount that makes a person stop and think. And if someone were to give that amount of money, with intention, I believe they would pay attention to where it went, what happened to it, and how it effected change. I wanted women to feel connected to their initial donation and for that connection to extend out to the grants it would fund; $1,000 seemed to be the right number.

As I was writing my new ideas down, it came to me that my goal was to create a model of giving that felt in sharp contrast to the "workplace campaigns" very much in vogue in the financial services industry. During these workplace campaign seasons, every employee received strong encouragement through all ranks of the bank's leadership to participate in this "painless" form of giving. Our donations would be made on a pre-tax basis, directly from our paychecks, "so we would never miss the money." We would also receive a pledge card upon which our "fair share" was identified as the percentage of our salary we were expected to give. All we had to do was sign the pledge form by the ascribed date and we could skip the meeting where the charity explained what they did and where your funds might go. Employees who did not comply could expect to hear from a manager who would explain how vital this giving was to the organization's culture—a culture that recognized and rewarded *team players*.

I had always cheerfully given to causes and even served as a campaign chair, but I certainly didn't feel connected to my gifts—automatically withdrawn from my account—and I knew my colleagues weren't feeling connected either. That seemed both sad and shortsighted for the charities in question. I knew from my own experience that I received far more satisfaction when I could see and understand the results of my giving. Even if only a small amount, knowing how my gift was activated to help was far more powerful than knowing I had given my fair share.

Reimagining connection

Coming together to give as a group was powerful, but there had to be a better way. As I reimagined giving, I recognized that $1,000 was a significant sum, but it wouldn't make a substantial impact when given to a nonprofit on its own. If we could gather at least one hundred women who *each* gave $1,000, and we pooled these funds together to offer the local nonprofit community grants of $100,000 or more, that would be significant. That would make a difference. We could design this new model as a pass-through foundation, where 100 percent of the funds donated each year would be pooled and given away without taking out a penny to cover administrative expenses.

This new way of giving had to be attractive to as many women as possible. I wanted to reach all women, not just a few in my community. I knew of a couple of "women's funds" that had started at the same time. They were poised to make a significant difference, but they had some characteristics that didn't resonate well with the women I knew. For example, money was going into these funds, but nothing was coming out. No donations were made to any nonprofits until the endowment fund target was met.

My goal, on the other hand, was to give away big grants immediately, without delay or feeling the need to retain an endowment. I felt it was important that the women who gave their $1,000 didn't have to wait long to see the power of their philanthropy.

Another limitation of these women's funds was that any grants awarded were made with a strict gender lens, ensuring the benefit was directed only at women's and girls' causes. Many women I spoke with viewed this type of funding lens as too narrow and could disqualify worthy nonprofits from receiving much-needed funding. I understood that most women and girls would benefit from a cure for prostate cancer or an equine therapy program for veterans suffering from PTSD, even if these were not projects that could ever qualify for a grant from a restricted women's fund.

As I reimagined a donor model, I also focused on recipients. Rather than prescribing where the donated funds would go, I hoped to encourage any qualified nonprofit to apply for our grants. I imagined five broad Focus Areas, where every woman could see her priorities represented, and every nonprofit would see that their mission qualified for consideration. The five Focus Areas I first envisioned, and that still hold true for most chapters today, are these:

- Arts & Culture
- Education
- Health & Wellness
- Family
- Environment

Creating the Impact100 model

I felt I had struck upon a simple yet powerful concept, one so simple that I was sure I was missing something. Perhaps there were reasons things couldn't be done this way? Surely that would explain why an organization like Impact100 didn't already exist. Were many organizations operating like this already? I was no expert, after all. I was just a banker who understood and appreciated the value of giving back to my community.

Fortunately, I had brilliant friends—women who had leadership experience in the nonprofit world, women who were lawyers, accountants, and trust officers. I started calling these smart and capable women. I needed to explain my big idea and have them tell me where my logic was wrong, or if I wasn't so wrong, I hoped they would connect me with the organizations that worked this way. Not only would I join them, but I also knew a bunch of women who would want to join them too! One by one, I made the calls, and one by one, women told me that I wasn't crazy. They said this was an idea worth pursuing, and they were eager to help launch it.

For this pass-through concept to be practical, I had to create an entirely different model from the traditional giving methods. Most of the time, when money is raised for a project, a donor can give at any time. It's never too late to provide financial support for a cause we care about. In order for my newly conceived concept to work, we would have to operate differently. The model I designed would give away every dollar women gave within the calendar year that they gave it, so we would need to inform the nonprofits about exactly how much money was available in our grants. To do so, we needed to create a calendar that included an annual giving (or membership) deadline. This element of the model could be a challenge for our members because it was unusual. The need for a membership deadline was a result of my determination to give away every dollar donated right away, rather than holding some donations or having a percentage of donations going toward administrative costs. Clear and frequent communication about how this giving model would work would be required. The last thing I wanted to do was to exclude or disappoint any potential members.

The way I designed the giving model, the cycle would begin with the women I was hoping to reach. To start, I would have to explain this concept and ask women to join by donating their $1,000 membership fee. The group of women I initially called to vet the idea with were invited to serve as the founding board. As a leadership team, we made our financial commitment first. As we started to spread the word by telling our friends, family, colleagues, and neighbors about this new way of giving, women soon understood the concept and committed to joining us. Excitedly, we kept a running total of committed members and a second list of those whose checks we had received. If this sounds redundant, bear with me. You see, a woman who commits to be a member is making a pledge or a promise to make the $1,000 donation. We certainly did not want to leave anyone out, but in order to "count" as a member, you needed to fully fund your $1,000 donation by a strict deadline.

Shortly after the membership deadline, we held an event called the "Big Reveal." This was when we celebrated all the women who had joined and announced to the community exactly how many members we had and how much money we had to give away. Because we give away 100 percent of the membership dues raised, we needed to have an exact accounting. At this event, the nonprofits in the area learned how big the grant would be—with the goal of reaching $100,000. The announcement was our word to the nonprofit community, and we needed to be fully confident that we could deliver on the promise of the Big Reveal. The amount announced was the exact amount we had received in membership payments.

From there, we held informational sessions for nonprofits to understand how our grant process worked, what our grant application contained, and our deadlines and additional requirements.

We also trained our members. Members had the choice whether to get involved. They didn't need any skills to volunteer, as we provided training on how to properly assess an application to ensure it was transformational and sustainable. Members were invited to make a site visit and score the pool of applicants in the Focus Area of their choice. Each Focus Area team and a special finance team completed a full review of all the applications, toward the goal of ultimately selecting one nonprofit applicant as that Focus Area's grant finalist.

The five finalists were then announced to the community, and a summary of their proposals was shared with members. Members receive enough information to truly understand each applicant's proposal before attending our Annual Meeting/Awards Celebration.

This grand finale event would become the most significant meeting of the year, where we would hear from our finalists and cast our votes. To ensure a level playing field among our nonprofit finalists, presenters followed strict guidelines as to timing, and no technology, handouts, or "party favors" would be allowed. Members cast their ballots and ultimately awarded the grant(s). The current year's grant cycle concluded at this event. Simultaneously, we officially kicked off membership recruiting for the next grant year.

And it worked!

That's how we set up the cycle in the beginning, and to my delight, it worked. To this day, we follow that model—which has been inspiring, powerful, and uplifting for all involved. It celebrates and connects each initial $1,000 donation to the critical work our collective $100,000+ will fund in a personal, tangible, and transformational way.

Now bear in mind, I did not have a pedigree or a strong background in nonprofit work. What I had was years of banking experience and the desire to empower women to transform the community. The miracle is that it actually worked! What I knew then, and know even better now, is that when there is a call to action for generosity, everyone benefits.

Giving circles

I rarely refer to Impact100 as a giving circle. This is intentional on my part, and a result of several factors. The first of which is that when

Impact100 was created, the term "giving circle" was not in the vernacular of the IRS.

When I was in the process of launching Impact100, I read several books and sought guidance from people who had launched funds of all kinds to learn how to begin. I eventually engaged the professional services of an attorney and accountant to file the necessary paperwork, but understanding what I was building felt vital to me. I read that philanthropic foundations fall into two separate and distinct categories: endowed and pass-through. Logically, an endowed foundation builds up a corpus or principal funds (called an endowment) from which to draw incremental amounts for grantmaking and operational expenses. In contrast, a pass-through foundation accepts donations but doesn't hold them. Instead, these donations flow through the foundation to fund grants and other expenses. Based on these terms, Impact100 is intentionally set up as a pass-through foundation.

Further, as the term "giving circle" became commonly used, the vast majority of giving circle organizations operated quite differently from Impact100. For example, there were large giving circle groups where women would gather over a meal and a bottle of wine to discuss different nonprofit organizations. By the end of the evening, they would select the nonprofit to whom they would give their money and make a gift. There is little process and therefore little follow-through or stewardship of these funds. In many cases, the giving circle itself is not a charitable organization. Instead, the members write their checks and make their donations directly to their nonprofit of choice.

There is certainly nothing wrong with this model, and I have benefited from my membership in giving circles like this. But when contrasted with the process of Impact100, both on the grant assessment or vetting side and on the grant follow-up and stewardship side, the term "giving circle" feels inaccurate in describing the work we do.

Most often, I describe Impact100 as a collective giving group or a pass-through foundation, which feels more accurate and reflective of our work. Impact100 is under the umbrella term of a giving circle but is set apart because of the thorough processes set in place.

To get an in-depth look at the essential processes of Impact100, please refer to the detailed Impact100 model found in the appendix.

> ## Increasing Your Impact
>
> This chapter tells the story of how the concept of Impact100 came about, along with some data on how women give and traditional giving opportunities. Impact100 was specifically designed to benefit women by removing the obstacles that kept too many women on the sidelines, not seeing a viable path to community service and philanthropy. Some of the features of the Impact100 model were very different from the mainstream.
>
> As a banker, I was an unlikely founder. Yet, I believe that being a bit of an "outsider" became my superpower. I wasn't limited by what "we have always done." I was solving a problem. Like the jigsaw puzzles I built with my grandmother as a child, I put the pieces together without knowing what the picture would look like. In the end, Impact100 was born.

5

What If?

> Every great dream begins with a dreamer. Always remember
> you have within you the strength, the patience, and the
> passion to reach for the stars to change the world.
>
> —Harriet Tubman

When I returned home from Michigan that summer after filling my spiral notebook with my ideas, I eagerly anticipated forming our new pass-through foundation—what we now know as Impact100. I had identified more than a dozen highly capable women in Cincinnati and was eager to launch this exciting new project.

Then, out of nowhere, on September 11, 2001, our country changed forever. Personally, I was shocked alongside the nation. I put everything related to Impact100 on hold. It was a devastating, heart-wrenching time—sad, scary, and uncertain. That one dreadful morning exposed our nation's vulnerability. We were grieving.

INVITATION TO IMPACT

As the months went by and the world began to find a new normal, my mind and heart kept going back to this new giving vehicle and wondering, *What if?* I felt compelled to find out whether we should move forward with Impact100. There was so much need all around me.

So many people were working tirelessly to help others. I knew they needed funding. I knew that the worried faces of my friends would brighten if they realized they had the power to effect positive change—that they had the power to make a difference together. They just needed a new model to make a greater impact. And I had that model.

So, on October 25, 2001, I invited the original fifteen women I had identified as potential founding board members to dinner. They knew they were coming to talk about this concept and to make some decisions about our future. What they didn't realize is that, in my mind, if at least ten of these women didn't feel invested in this idea, excited about building it, and committed to the outcome, I likely wouldn't be able to move forward with Impact100.

I understood very well that although this idea came from me, executing it well would take a village. And I knew that the women sitting around that dinner table had the skills, experience, and network connections I lacked. For this concept to succeed, I would need at least ten of us joining together to build this brand-new venture. So, when we gathered that evening, we explored the idea.

Ultimately, I had to ask the hard questions: Is now the right time to launch Impact100? Are we the right people? It felt important to know the answers, especially in light of 9/11. As it turned out, everyone was in agreement that night. If not now, when? If not us, who? Well, when I left dinner that evening, all fifteen women had committed to helping launch Impact100. At this same dinner, we decided on the name and determined some of the other technical details that would help us launch.

Getting off the ground

The first step was filing for our 501(c)3, which was approved in March of 2002. Once we were officially a nonprofit, we actively started spreading the word about Impact100. In our grassroots recruiting efforts, we had one-on-one conversations with as many women as we could find.

We actively searched for a diverse group of women, pursuing members from outside of our professions and neighborhoods. For Impact100 to reach its full potential, we had to reach as many women as possible. All women were, and still are, welcome. If we wanted Impact100 to reach its fullest potential, we needed to attract women from all walks of life and every demographic. The best way to do that would be to have a wide variety of groups represented on our leadership team.

In those early days, we would try to speak about Impact100 at a gathering of women, rather than reaching only one or two people at a time. The concept was so new that it took a bit of work for us to articulate how our program operated. By sharing the idea in a larger group, we began to see our membership numbers climb. We shared the vision and the model, asking people to join us. We set a goal of reaching one hundred women by May. In my mind, if we couldn't get one hundred women to commit in a town this size and using the networks of this group of women who were so well connected, then I feared we should not do it at all. But by May, we had received checks from 123 women. We had a whopping $123,000 to give away!

By our current standards for an Impact100 launch, 123 members is a pretty small amount. But back then, this was a brand-new concept, and what we were attempting had not been done before. So, that 123 number was a monumental achievement in our eyes. We were over the moon. We were, however, building the airplane as we were flying.

Once the $123,000 was in the bank, we immediately turned our focus to training our nonprofits and encouraging them to apply for our grant.

We had several information sessions where we announced to the nonprofits how many members we had, and therefore how much money we had to give away, explaining how they could apply. We walked the nonprofits through our grant application process so they would know what to expect. It seems counterintuitive given the significant grant we were offering, but nonprofit leaders needed encouragement to apply for the funds.

In our first year, we received more than one hundred nonprofit applications across our five Focus Areas. Thankfully, we had many volunteers who signed up to serve on the Focus Area Committees (FACs) and the financial review team. The Focus Area Committees were busy. Impact100 members who volunteered were trained, and the applications were carefully vetted. Each FAC team discussed and analyzed each proposal carefully, asking questions for confirmation or to fill in gaps. As we began identifying site visit candidates, the finance committee reviewed every possible finalist to ensure financial viability. Once the site visits were complete, each team determined the one finalist organization they would recommend.

The Annual Awards Celebration at the Annual Meeting would be the culmination of the entire Impact100 grant cycle and the year's most significant event. Each finalist would pitch their project live at the event to be the recipient of the inaugural Impact100 transformational grant. The finalists would have only a microphone and a podium. We would have a strict time limit of ten minutes for each presentation and would not allow any technical support or handouts of any kind. The idea was to level the playing field so each applicant would shine based on the merits of their proposal and not because of a glitzy tech display or clever party favor.

What If?

As the leadership team began the planning of the Annual Meeting and Awards Celebration, we thought through every detail. The board talked about the flow of the events and tried to anticipate every scenario ahead of time. If done well, this event would be the highlight of the Impact100 grant cycle. We needed to allow time for socializing and networking, uninterrupted presentation time for our finalists, performance reports on the work of Impact100, along with voting and dinner.

We worried that when the votes were tallied by the outside CPA firm engaged to count and certify the vote, and the grant recipient was announced, everyone on stage would end up crying—the nonprofits that did not get funded would be crying; the nonprofit that *did* get funded would be crying. All this crying would upset or rattle our members who, instead of feeling inspired by the transformational gift they were a part of, would be rather concerned, even sad, at the turn of events. This undesirable outcome came to be known internally as a "Miss America moment."

Because of that potential dramatic scene, we did our first Annual Meeting differently. We did not announce our grant recipient at the event. Instead, I called each finalist the next morning and shared the outcome of the vote. Each finalist did an excellent job and submitted outstanding proposals, making voting difficult for each member. History was made that day in September of 2002 when our membership voted to give our first grant to the McMicken Dental Clinic in Over-the-Rhine. Once all the nonprofits were notified, we sent an email out to our membership announcing our inaugural grant recipient, the McMicken Dental Clinic.

In hindsight, our plan was flawed, because those phone calls the next day were tricky—or at least four out of the five were. I needed to take care to call the four finalists who were not chosen and give them the bad news before calling our grant recipient. I also had to be careful to ensure that none of this had the opportunity to leak until we were ready with our press release and an email to our members.

I made all those calls the next day, and we were in business. During the debrief of the event with the leadership team, we determined that our fears of a stage full of crying nonprofit professionals were unfounded. In the future, rather than delaying notification of the outcome of the vote, we would celebrate the grant recipient at the event itself. It has worked wonderfully.

"Stop and think" gifts

One of the most important decisions I had faced when developing the model for Impact100 was determining the size of each individual member's contribution. While my goal was to empower women to give to their communities, asking for too much or too little by way of a donation was a surefire way to see both women and their communities disappointed with the results.

By asking for $1,000 from one hundred members, we ensure that the grants we offer in most communities where Impact100 works are among the most sizeable available to area nonprofits. Donations this large allow an agency to fully execute a program, dream big, and try something new. The size of our grants is a vital part of the Impact100 model. These grants are meant to be substantial, transformational, and sustainable.

The power of pooling our resources to fund something big has always attracted women to join our work and nonprofits to apply for our grants. Although for many members, the initial donation to Impact100 was the first time they had ever given a gift of $1,000 to a single nonprofit, the notion of being a part of a gift of $100,000 or more is life changing.

I often get asked about revising the annual membership fee to a lesser amount of $500, for example. The concept is well-intended. For many women, the reasoning goes that $1,000 is too much. Offering the option of either a full $1,000 membership or a half-membership of $500 would provide better access to women for whom the $1,000 is out of reach. Members paying the full amount of $1,000 would receive one vote and those contributing $500 would receive a half vote. All members can—and are encouraged to—participate in the Focus Area grant review teams and volunteer in other capacities.

The idea comes from a good place but often brings unintended consequences. We see that in many instances, women who could afford to pay the full membership have no incentive to do so and make a gift of $500 instead. Feeling less connected to their gift, their connection to the work of Impact100 diminishes as well, making member retention a challenge. Even if the option results in more women joining an Impact100 chapter, the impact to the community is diluted as the grant pool is reduced, resulting in less money available to the worthy nonprofits in the area.

Having met Impact100 members from around the globe, I have heard the pride in the voices of members who share how they budgeted weekly to afford their membership. Each person has a unique story, but I have heard of members who skip their designer coffee stops, limit meals out, park in a parking lot a bit farther away from their office, and stash five-dollar bills in an "Impact100" envelope until they gather the funds to make their membership payment.

For some Impact100 members, the act of calculating, budgeting, and intentionally setting aside money to fund the coming year's Impact100 membership seems to provide almost as much joy as giving away the $100,000 grant at the end of the grant cycle. I believe being so thoughtful consistently throughout the year truly boosts the oxytocin blast that generosity brings. We really do feel good when we give, and these actions result in additional opportunities to bask in the glow of giving.

Another way to make the $1,000 membership amount more accessible is to allow installment payments. This opportunity encourages members to determine a schedule of saving that works best with their unique situation while regularly setting aside funds specifically for this purpose. Several Impact100 chapters allow or even encourage members to fund their annual membership via a monthly giving program. A campaign that consistently catches my attention is the way Impact100 Metro Detroit promotes this option. They call upon women in the community to give monthly to create a "lifetime of impact." What a powerful message and way to position a monthly giving option.

Offering partial scholarships/matching grants to women that matches their contribution with funds provided by another allows the member to pay a lower amount without diluting the impact of her membership. Ideally, these scholarships could be offered in two ways: First is a one-year 50–50 match where the member pays $500, and the matching grant pays the remaining $500. This type of opportunity is best for members who are able to make the full contribution but have an extenuating circumstance or limited time to make the full contribution prior to the chapter's membership deadline. It makes the assumption that the member can make the next year's full membership payment on her own.

Alternatively, offering a step-up matching grant works to instill a habit of budgeting our resources and our time to allow for consistent philanthropic contribution. It is a four-year experience that begins with the member paying $350, and the grant paying $650. In year two, the member and the matching grant each pay $500. By year three, the member pays $650, and the match is $350. By year four, the member pays the full $1,000. Each year, the member not only contributes more financially but also gives more of her time. The benefits to the member and the organization are manifold, as this approach strengthens the philanthropy "muscle" of the member, a practice that will benefit her for her lifetime.

I am not so naive to believe that everyone can make a gift of $1,000 each year, but having met women from a wide variety of financial capacities, I am convinced offering a two-tiered membership is a flawed approach.

Overhead aversion

Interestingly, one of the most important facets of the Impact100 model is the idea that 100 percent of a member's $1,000 donation goes directly to the charity in the form of a significant grant, with nothing taken out to cover administrative expenses. As I mentioned earlier, this is to address the lack of transparency and trust in the non-profit sector due to a small number of bad actors who have selfishly abused the system.

Impact100 membership can be the first significant gift for many of the women who join. Making the math clean, giving all of each member's donation, removes hesitancy in many of our members' minds. Once the member gets involved in the grant review process, becomes acquainted with local nonprofit leaders, and gains additional understanding of the realities of their work, most members fully support the idea of allowing some amount of the dollars raised to cover the infrastructure of the organization.

Notably, members with more philanthropic experience often join as 110 percent members, funding administrative costs with their additional $100 donation, or they simply donate additional funds to cover these costs as needs arise.

Personally, I agree with a premise made popular by Dan Pallotta's 2013 TED talk, "The Way We Think about Charity Is Dead Wrong," that we operate nonprofits and for-profits with two entirely different sets of rules—rules that penalize nonprofits and hamper their growth. For example, no one thinks twice if a for-profit CEO earns a seven-figure salary with stock options and bonuses. By contrast, if a nonprofit leader earned anything close to that, they would be scrutinized as being greedy and out of touch with the community they serve. When for-profit companies want to grow their revenues, they spend thousands of dollars on a compelling marketing campaign. Nonprofits do not typically have the budget to spend much on marketing, and if they did, charity rating agencies would score them badly as not stewarding donations well.

These differences (and so many more) in how we evaluate different types of organizations work against the nonprofit sector in myriad ways. Attracting top talent for nonprofit work is difficult with such a vast pay disparity. This means, in many cases, only people with a financial safety net in place can afford to work in the sector. Job seekers are put in a position to choose between a low-paying job at a cause they may be passionate about and a high-paying job at a for-profit corporation, and simply donating to the nonprofit.

For nonprofits, growing solely based on finding and asking donors to support your work is made all the more difficult when your organization is underfunded and understaffed. Access to a strong, compelling advertising and marketing campaign could result in significant gains in funding, rather than small, incremental increases.

I am fascinated by a relatively small study published in 2014 called "Avoiding Overhead Aversion in Charity."[9] The study concludes that when overhead expenses are covered by another donor, gifts to the charity increase more significantly than they do when other traditional incentives such as matching grants are offered. In my experience, these findings ring true. Although the notion of increasing the impact of a donation through a matching donor's generosity can be a powerful motivator, giving with the knowledge that 100 percent of your donation will go directly to the program or project you are funding is even more convincing.

When founder Scott Harrison built the nonprofit Charity: Water, his design included the premise that 100 percent of all public donations would go to build wells and provide clean drinking water in developing countries. As outlined on the nonprofit's website, from the beginning, the overhead expenses were covered by a small group of generous donors referred to as the Well. This approach was rather novel, and perhaps a bit risky, but this organization continues to raise incredible amounts of money to provide clean drinking water to those in need. Harrison felt when he launched, as I did when I designed Impact100, that removing the barrier of funding administrative expenses would encourage more people to give generously. This decision means we also need to cover our infrastructure costs with contributions from donors who understand our mission and want to support the work in a powerful way.

Selecting a grantee

All Impact100 grants are assessed using two significant lenses: Will the proposed project or program be transformational? And is it

---

9   Uri Gneezy, Elizabeth A. Keenan, and Ayelet Gneezy, "Avoiding Overhead Aversion in Charity," *Science* 346, no. 6209 (October 2014): 632–35, https://www.science.org/doi/10.1126/science.1253932.

sustainable? "Transformation" is an overused buzzword in philanthropy and carries many definitions. For Impact100, transformation includes a firm commitment to the unique needs of the community. We hope to fund significant change, rather than incremental progress, to address the community's most pressing problems. When we combine an intimate understanding of the problem with a significant grant, we're able to fund local solutions that produce transformational outcomes.

When it comes to funding a sustainable grant, we assess the program or project along with the viability of the nonprofit applicant itself. Exploring what kind of financial supports are likely to be available after our grant dollars have been spent, as well as the strength and capabilities of the leadership team, factors into our assessments. Each Focus Area grant review team takes their role to steward and protect our members' donations seriously. Our chosen grant recipient must be better off after receiving our funding.

The first-ever Impact100 grant was $123,000, and after I finished those difficult phone calls, the grant awarded to McMicken Dental Clinic brought new life to an underused but critical health provider. The grant funding replaced five old, unreliable dental chairs with five brand-new setups.

When the chairs were installed, the entire Impact100 membership was invited to tour the facility and see our investment in action. It turns out that a local family foundation decided to join our efforts. They funded fresh paint, new carpet, and office furniture to spruce up the office. Combined, these gifts created a total transformation for the clinic. It was wonderful that the family recognized the work we had done and wanted to be a part of the lasting transformation of a great organization. This early external validation of our work in grantmaking was an unexpected bonus.

As we toured the facility, easels placed around the room displayed before-and-after pictures, and this is where we saw the transformational work of the clinic. Each photoset contained two images of the same person, shown side by side. In the first set of images, we saw hardly any smiles except a few with black or missing teeth. The shame and anguish in the patients' eyes were painfully obvious. Next to these images were pictures of these same people, beaming. With their conditions fixed and their teeth restored or replaced, the dental patients' eyes shone with hope.

Because the clinic became a state-of-the-art facility, after the grant they began a program with Ohio State University School of Dentistry. Fourth-year dental students got "out" of the school's clinics and came to the clinic to do "real-life dental work" on people who needed it the most. It was a win-win for both programs, and this partnership became a model for other dental schools in this country. Judi became an adjunct professor at three different dental schools: Ohio State, Louisville School of Dentistry in Kentucky, and ATSU Arizona School of Dentistry and Oral Health.

Dr. Judith "Judi" Allen was the staff dentist who happily brought us on a tour around her facility. She invited me into her office to share another unexpected benefit of our funding: The calendar she used to schedule volunteer dentists was now full! Because of the new equipment, dentists were volunteering in her clinic. Judi had been working for years to get them to come, but they would nod, smile, and never actually volunteer. The clinic's old equipment was unreliable, and dentists didn't feel comfortable taking the risk of working with faulty equipment. Once the dentists knew they could trust the equipment, they were eager to support this underserved population. In addition, many of her former students came back to McMicken to volunteer, further growing the capacity of the small clinic.

The goal of every Impact100 grant is to be transformational and sustainable, and this grant had both elements in spades. The five new dental chairs created a ripple effect: the donation of new office equipment, a more dignified dental care experience for those in need, and consistent volunteer dentists contributing to the effort.

Getting the word out to nonprofits

That first year, and every year since, I've learned the lesson that an Impact100 chapter is only as powerful as the women who join and as transformational as the nonprofits who apply. It would be easy to assume that once an Impact100 chapter attracts one hundred or more members, the applications would come flooding in. After all, in many communities, our grants are the largest grant offerings available to nonprofits. Even in cases where we are not the largest funder, nonprofits need to be educated about our grant process and encouraged to apply.

We educate nonprofits in a number of ways. Impact100 chapters are encouraged to publicize the grant application process broadly and offer several nonprofit training sessions to address questions to ensure the nonprofits understand our process and timelines. The key is to be proactive and reach out to the nonprofit community to invite their participation. This includes direct emails as well as press releases directed at funding partners like local community foundations, Jewish Federations, family foundations, United Way chapters, and others.

Although it may seem counterintuitive, nonprofit applicants must be recruited and pursued in the same way members are. Inviting grant applications while explaining that the goal is to ultimately fund as many projects as possible each year helps to establish an expectation that benefits the entire community.

As a recruitment tool, it's hard to beat good, old-fashioned word of mouth. Since receiving that first grant, Dr. Judi Allen has become a dear friend of mine, and of Impact100 as well, joining the following year and renewing her membership every year since. She has been so inspired that she recruits new members to join Impact100 and is always willing to speak with nonprofits to encourage them to apply for a grant.

> ## Increasing Your Impact
>
> By asking, "What if?" we open our minds to new ideas and the potential for new realities. To be successful, it is important to fully understand the current landscape while imagining a better tomorrow. Wishing or hoping things were different will not make them so. Instead, we need to work with what we have and tirelessly seek to change the status quo.
>
> Success in launching Impact100 came because a large group of diverse and highly capable women came together to fund significant grants in their local community. Impact100 is powerful because so many viable nonprofits applied for our grants and dreamed big. The mission has been effective because we all spread the word and invited others to join in this important work.

6

Newsworthy

> I raise up my voice not so I can shout, but so that those without a voice can be heard.
>
> —Malala Yousafzai

As we were launching the first Impact100 in Cincinnati in 2001 and 2002, we reached out to the various local media outlets with press releases, emails, and phone calls in hopes of getting assistance in spreading the word to potential Impact100 members as well as potential grant applicants. The press was not too receptive to our requests. We received a small story here or there, but more often than not, our requests were declined or we never got a response at all.

Imagine my surprise when my home phone rang one afternoon and the woman on the other end of the line introduced herself as Lorna Grisby, the Midwest Deputy Bureau Chief for *People* magazine. After we had given our inaugural grant of $123,000 to the

INVITATION TO IMPACT

McMicken Dental Clinic, *The Cincinnati Enquirer* had run a small story announcing our funding. Lorna had read that story and was preparing to pitch her editor a story about the people behind the grassroots organizations around the country that were changing people's lives for the better. She needed some additional information for her pitch, hence the call to me. We had a lovely conversation and she promised to let me know, one way or the other, how her editor responded to the story idea.

A couple of weeks later, I heard back from Lorna. She told me that while her editor wasn't interested in the broad, round-up approach Lorna had prepared, the editor liked my story best. She said, "The entire article will be about you and your work with Impact100."

Over the coming weeks, Lorna and I spent lots of time together on the phone. She asked me questions about my past, about my family, and what it was like growing up. Lorna didn't just interview me, either. She interviewed my father, my sister, the leadership at the McMicken Dental Clinic, and even some Impact100 members. We spent hours on the phone and in-person as she asked an unending stream of questions.

She explained that to get an article to run in *People*, she would have to write a lengthy piece—one that could be up to thirty pages—based on all her research and reporting on me and Impact100. Then, in *People*'s stratified system, a writer in New York, followed by several editors, would ultimately whip the story into an article appropriate for *People*. I was nervous: She asked so many personal questions that seemed unrelated to my work at Impact100. I couldn't imagine why she needed all this background, and sharing my story with a stranger, even this charming one, was often uncomfortable.

Lorna talked about the fact-checking process. She had to independently validate every fact, so she checked and double-checked everything I told her with other sources to be sure that what she would ultimately put in print would be truthful. This was more challenging for me than she could have guessed. Early in our interview, she asked about my family, childhood, and parents. When I told her that my mother had died when I was a girl, she asked about the circumstances of her death. For years, I had never told the real story of how my mother died. And here I was being interviewed by *People*—the most widely subscribed publication at the time. I was afraid to tell the truth and yet equally terrified not to.

I couldn't imagine lying in print. So, for the first time in my adult life, I told Lorna Grisby that my mother had taken her own life after struggling with depression for many years. I begged her not to make this detail a primary aspect of the story she was writing. I also requested to approve anything she wrote before it went to print. She laughed a little and said no one, no matter who they were, gets to approve a *People* story before it hits the newsstand, so she was sorry, but I would have to wait and read what she wrote until it was published. That realization was terrifying.

Lorna came to Cincinnati to do some additional reporting, and so did one of the magazine's photographers. He had a list of pictures he wanted to take, including a photo of me with my kids, and several shots at the McMicken Dental Clinic. The most important picture, he said, was a group shot with as many members of Impact100 as I could gather on short notice. This image would have to be so compelling that it would entice the reader to read this story, rather than skimming through to something more interesting.

As he set up the photo, the photographer had me stand on a slightly elevated platform, pretending to be writing a check, looking over my shoulder back beyond the camera. Impact100 members were staged all around me, and each one was reaching out, trying to hand me their check. The photo setup felt awkward and unnatural. Impact100 was about removing barriers to giving that prevented women in Cincinnati from being involved in their community. It was about generosity and community service and transformational grants. It was about helping our nonprofits do the vital work they carried out heroically for our neediest neighbors. The staging of this photo felt out of sync with the purpose and spirit of Impact100. I tried to explain why I didn't think it was the right image, but the photographer insisted he knew what he was doing. As with the other photos, he moved around, adjusted lighting, repositioned people, and captured several images in quick succession. When he was satisfied, he assured me that the pictures were great and to trust the experts at the magazine to get it right. It ended up being the central photo of the piece.

Parallel universe

It was also the summer of 2001 when my marriage of fifteen years hit a major stumbling block. At first, we sought therapy and tried to salvage our marriage. By the following year, we separated, with the assurance that divorce was the only realistic course of action. As Impact100 was forming and thriving, my marriage was faltering and ultimately failing. This was an incredibly difficult realization for me.

You see, I have always defined myself as the kind of person who stays married, who works it out and keeps the family together. To be clear, I had close friends whose marriages had ended in divorce and never considered those outcomes to be anything other than appropriate and even honorable. Yet somehow those same standards didn't apply to me. I worried about the kids and how they would be affected. I did a great deal of soul-searching as I tried to figure out who I really was and whether the marriage could be saved.

Ultimately, with the help of experts, therapists, and supportive family and friends, I knew that divorce was the best course of action for all concerned. We followed the guidance from experts to make it as easy on our children as we possibly could. The kids and I went to family therapy together. Although often uncomfortable, these regular conversations truly helped us all articulate our feelings in real time and work through this time of difficult transition.

People hits the newsstands

The *People* magazine article featuring Impact100 had originally been scheduled to hit the newsstands over the 2002 holiday season. I cannot remember the exact reason anymore, but the Impact100 article was delayed until January 2003.

Before the issue came out, I called my sisters and warned them that the truth of how our mother died might be included in the article. I also spoke to close friends, sharing the story so they would hear it from me and not from an article, told in a way I may or may not feel comfortable with. This was a huge part of my past I didn't readily share out of concern that my mother—and I, by extension—would be judged based solely on this one data point, without an understanding of the full picture. Admittedly, at this stage of my life, that picture was one I couldn't fully understand myself. Ultimately, *People* magazine did not sensationalize my mother's death, but they did include it. Toward the end of the article, her depression, addiction, and suicide were mentioned in the context of recognizing that you do not always know what people have gone through.

I was so focused on how the story would be told and what the images might reflect that it never occurred to me what the story might *inspire*. After the magazine came out, I was wholly unprepared for the positive reaction. I received a constant flow of emails and phone calls from people hoping to replicate Impact100 in their communities.

I replied to every email and phone call I received. I was so thrilled that this idea was not only removing the barriers for women in Cincinnati, but it was now poised to make a powerful difference for women in countless communities. Women needed to find a viable path to community service and philanthropy in their backyard. I was overwhelmed but delighted to imagine that this giving model would reach well beyond the seven hills of this beautiful city I called home.

I was asked by many whether they could buy an Impact100 franchise or a license to operate an Impact100 organization in their local area. Well-meaning friends and colleagues suggested I charge a fee to make some money from this idea, but it made no sense to me. Impact100 was created to remove barriers, not build them. Charging a fee would simply serve to gatekeep which communities were able to experience this potentially life-changing pathway to giving back.

In the wake of Impact100's appearance in *People*, the two communities that were most eager to bring our giving model to their hometowns were Austin, Texas, and Pensacola, Florida. I spent hours on the phone with the founding leadership of both new chapters. They loved the idea and were excited to see what it would do for women and their community.

I often say that the Impact100 model is simple, but executing it well is not easy. I was eager to freely share exactly how the Impact100 model worked and why each element was designed the way it was, but I felt certain that aspects of the work needed to be done by the local founding board. Just as part of the model calls for a "stop and think" gift of $1,000 to ensure that each member feels connected and is mindful of her part in the $100,000+ grants made, the leadership team also needed to wrestle through some of the policies and practices that went into creating bylaws and other governing documents. This investment of time and discussion had a value of its own. It helped build connection, clarify intent, and develop a cohesive leadership team.

An unexpected benefit of that magazine article

One more phone call I received in the wake of the *People* magazine article would change my life. A call came from the past that I never expected—from a guy named Rick Steele.

Back when I was about sixteen years old and in high school, I met a boy while I was waterskiing with friends on Walloon Lake in Northern Michigan. We dated casually that summer, and for a couple of summers after that. Each August, returning to our homes in different states, we would write a few letters back and forth but resume dating other people in our hometowns. We lost track of each other after college began and life moved on.

It turns out that all these years later, while sitting in the waiting room for his annual physical, he'd picked up a magazine and begun to flip the pages when an image caused him to stop and read the article. He had a split second of recognition and read on to confirm his suspicions. As he read the article, it was clear the photo he recognized was mine, prompting the initial call. Hearing his voice that day, I instantly recognized it as the voice of my former beau.

The *People* article had briefly mentioned my ex-husband, making it clear I was single. As for me, enough time had passed and I was ready to entertain the idea of dating again. I wasn't sure what to expect, but

I remembered Rick as a kind, trustworthy, and great guy—certainly a more inviting possibility than the men some of my well-meaning friends and neighbors wanted to introduce me to. After Rick and I reconnected, some friends gave me the book *My Boyfriend's Back* by Donna Hanover. As I read the many stories of rediscovering past love, I realized the intangible sense of trust and ease I felt with Rick is a common experience among couples who reunite after a relationship earlier in life. I knew who he'd been as a teenager, and as I got to know the man he had become, my affection deepened and our relationship became stronger.

We were engaged in November of 2004, and on June 4, 2005, my oldest kids, Stephen and Alex, escorted me down the aisle, following my daughter, Hailey, and Rick's daughter, Brooke, as our maids of honor. Jake, Rick's youngest, had the responsibility of delivering the rings to us at the altar. Although Rick and I took a mini-honeymoon of just three days, it was our family honeymoon to Arizona that felt like the real celebration of our vows as one big family.

Thanks in part to *People* magazine, we are a happily blended family of five remarkable kids.

More than Impact100

The article in *People* magazine did more than launch the Impact100 movement. After the article hit the newsstands, I was asked to be interviewed on local TV. I was on the cover of *Cincinnati Woman* magazine with an in-depth story about the work of Impact100. I was even asked to speak to a group of students studying nonprofit leadership at Northern Kentucky University. These were opportunities I gladly embraced, knowing it would help bring more women to Impact100, and to giving in general.

I heard from a church that had used the *People* article as the basis for a Sunday sermon. I heard from friends and former colleagues who read the story and reached out to tell me how wonderful and powerful they found this model to be. Hearing what this idea meant to so many people from all walks of life was a gratifying whirlwind, and it was beautifully unexpected.

People magazine had introduced the concept of Impact100 to a wide variety of people in cities around the globe. As Impact100 chapters started to launch, word spread further as women shared their experience with the model with sisters, mothers, daughters, and friends. I was contacted by so many who wanted to replicate the model and learn the best way to be successful. Other communities even took the idea and created something new by pulling out the pieces of the Impact100 model that resonated best and combining them with their own visions of collective giving, designed to suit their local communities.

As word spread about Impact100, the growth began. The next two chapters started in Pensacola, Florida, and Austin, Texas, which each gifted their initial grants in 2004. By 2006, seven chapters were awarding grants, and by 2012, we had doubled to fourteen. By 2016, the Impact100 movement would more than double that number, reaching thirty-four communities around the globe. Regardless of the strength of the economy, the Impact100 model continues to grow. Perhaps not surprisingly, at the height of a global pandemic, nine new chapters launched during 2020 alone.

As I write this, in 2022, we currently have more than sixty-five Impact100 chapters and requests from over fifty communities around the globe hoping to launch a new chapter.

Increasing Your Impact

Without a doubt, Impact100 would not have grown so quickly were it not for the story in *People* magazine. Understanding the profound power of the press is vital to furthering your message, regardless of the subject matter. It is not easy or predictable, but a well-placed story can change the trajectory of your organization, and your life, if you let it.

It is not easy to get the attention of the press in hopes of sharing your story. Since our inception, the pressure on journalists in every form of media has only increased, making it even more difficult to become "newsworthy." Keep reaching out and keep doing the work. That is the best plan I know for success.

I am forever grateful to *People* and every other media outlet that has chosen to tell our story of Impact100.

7

Transformation

> We should all do something to right the wrongs that
> we see and not just complain about them.
>
> —Jacqueline Kennedy Onassis

For generations, we have been interpreting the Golden Rule—"do unto others as you would have them do unto you"—too literally. Today, most people understand it to mean they should aspire to treat others exactly the way they want to be treated. When most people give gifts to friends and loved ones, for example, they're most likely to give something that they want for themselves. This phenomenon is so widespread, marketers even use it to their advantage by encouraging shoppers to "give one to get one" for themselves during holiday promotions.

Tony Alessandra and Michael O'Connor proposed an alternative to the Golden Rule, called the Platinum Rule, which they define in their 1996 book of the same name: "Do unto others as they'd like done unto them."[10] The adjustment in perspective required to follow this Platinum Rule is subtle but doubtlessly impactful for the gift receiver.

In my own life, I have been guilty of misinterpreting the Golden Rule more often than I care to admit. Two clear examples spring to mind—my sister and my husband. In the case of my sister, Tina, we have similar tastes in clothing and décor. Shopping with and for Tina is always fun. There is one significant difference between us: I am a sentimentalist and connect certain objects with the persons or places they came from. Receiving another scarf, serving dish, candle, or sweater is a bonus to me. I love having options, and keeping a collection of things I love makes me happy.

Tina, on the other hand, is decidedly minimalist. Clutter makes her uncomfortable, and in her world, there is absolutely no reason to have several iterations of the same item. A duplicate scarf, to her, is unnecessary and wasteful. For years, as much as I hate to admit it, this significant difference between us simply never sank in for me. I have given her a variety of serving dishes, decorative artifacts, and tchotchkes of all types, just because they were pretty or quirky or fun. Always gracious, she received them well, but when the next occasion came around, she politely reminded me that she truly didn't need or want anything. We have since resolved this issue by shopping together for each other's birthdays, a tradition that is much more fun and successful than my shopping unsupervised.

But then there is my husband, Rick, an engineer and a consummate "guy's guy." He makes things, fixes things, invents things, and is happiest working in a well-equipped and organized garage. His

---

10   Tony Alessandra, PhD, and Michael J. O'Connor, PhD, *The Platinum Rule: Discover the Four Basic Business Personalities—And How They Can Lead You to Success* (New York: Warner Books, 1996).

favorite stores sell tools and power equipment. Early in our courtship and marriage, after noticing that Rick never wore a watch, I was certain it was because he never had a nice one. So I bought him one. When he did not wear it that often, I tried again—and again. Each time my jeweler and I were certain we had totally nailed Rick's style. Each time when he didn't wear the watch, it seemed again that we were way off base. My husband is so nice, it was years before he finally confessed that he simply did not care for jewelry.

Over the years, we have become better givers because we have learned to observe and appreciate each other's preferences.

Learning to align your gift giving

Too often the gifts we give others miss the mark because we base our purchases on faulty assumptions about the recipient. This is more common than we might want to believe. Why? Because we often choose gifts for those we love with our own preferences in mind, rather than their preferences.

If we make mistakes giving to our most intimate friends and family, how do we expect to give well to people, communities, and causes we do not know nearly as well? Sometimes, whether we realize it or not, our gifts and good intentions can fall short when we try to help those in great need. This kind of miscalculation can happen for a number of reasons, but let us turn our attention to three of the most common causes.

1. Decisions based only on partial information

As people gain experience giving to the causes they care about, there is a tendency to ask fewer questions as experience begins to automatically fill in the blanks in new circumstances, applying past lessons from other projects and outcomes to the current one. For the most part, this is an efficient practice and makes great sense. In most cases, there is no need to "reinvent the wheel," as the saying goes.

In some situations, though, our rush to efficiency can backfire. After only a cursory examination, we can be too quick to reach a conclusion—and therefore, a philanthropic decision—before fully understanding the unique circumstances of each situation. Understanding local cultures, engaging the proper stakeholders, and respecting the unique story of a community or nonprofit are all invaluable data points to direct better outcomes. Seeking to fully understand the whole picture before jumping in with ready-made solutions will improve the efficacy of our generosity.

Part of what makes Impact100 so powerful is the reliance upon local leaders. At every point in the Impact100 process, the members in the local community identify the most pressing problems while assessing the solutions presented in grant applications. As an independent donor, it helps to have a process or system in place when assessing potential funding partners. By slowing down your decision-making (even if only slightly), you will likely see a disproportionate benefit of knowledge that will save you from making philanthropic decisions without sufficient information.

2. Stubborn problems demand complex, creative interventions

Some of the problems we face today are entrenched and complicated. Understanding and opening our thoughts to creative resolution is vital to strong, effective philanthropy. The right solution may stretch our nonprofit organizations in new ways. Sometimes, collaborations or partnerships bring the best solutions, but this is not always easy or comfortable for the partnering organizations.

Seek first to understand and then to be understood. As philanthropists, we must be sure we fully understand the problem at hand and all of its contributing factors before we jump in to fix it.

Jamie Van Leeuwen founded an organization I admire called the Global Livingston Institute (GLI) in East Africa in 2009, after visiting Uganda and Rwanda and seeing firsthand the many times solutions were delivered in East Africa before the needs were fully understood. Underpinning the work of GLI is the mantra "Listen. Think. Act."

This deliberate and thoughtful process has been a game-changer for the work of GLI and the people it supports. This deceptively simple concept provides a vital road map to successful philanthropy and intervention.

3. When all you have is a hammer, everything looks like a nail

Every philanthropist has her limits and preferences, and most identify a "sweet spot" of giving that becomes a favorite vehicle—say, donating wish-list items or organizing volunteer groups with friends. For many philanthropists, this makes great sense and is efficient. As new requests come in, we assess them in light of our favorite tool. After all, we had success with our "hammer" and now we want to hammer everyone.

I see this often with families who enjoy volunteering together. They approach nonprofits who are doing great work and request a "done in a day," efficient experience for multiple generations of their family to participate in together. From the family's perspective, this makes sense. The agency will get five to seven people working four to six hours together to complete a project. The family even brings its own supplies, further blessing the agency and its clients in a powerful way.

For many nonprofits, this represents a remarkable gift that they will eagerly facilitate. For others, it can be an awkward intrusion, disrupting the privacy of their clients or the schedules of an already overworked staff. Some nonprofits are simply not designed to support volunteers. When all we have is a hammer, we often do not understand being turned down, because we cannot see that the agency instead needs a wrench.

This principle can also be applied to financial gifts. Some generous philanthropists get attached to a giving vehicle like crowdfunding on social media or matching grants. These tactics are effective for agencies with strong, established donors and a robust social media platform, but are almost impossible for early stage nonprofits without a deep bench of donors at the ready. To avoid this syndrome, ask the nonprofits what type of support they need before deciding what to give. Obtaining this guidance will make you a better giver, and the gift you make will deliver better results based on realistic expectations.

If asking a nonprofit what they need feels vulnerable, remember, you can always turn them down if it is out of your wheelhouse. And who knows? Maybe their request will be easier or require less money than you might have offered. Creative solutions that serve both the agency and the community become possible when you stop trying to give others what you want and take the time to learn what it is that they actually need.

Increasing Your Impact

The word "philanthropy" comes from two Greek words, "philos," which means "love," and "anthropos," which means "mankind or humanity." So, philanthropy can be understood as a love for humanity. This definition has prompted me over the years to encourage all people who give to describe themselves as "philanthropists." Words, labels, and names matter. Connecting your heart and your mind to your giving will do wonders to improve your outcomes.

As you are building your philanthropic muscle, do not apologize for asking questions. It demonstrates your humility and willingness to learn and will make your gifts more impactful.

8

Million-Dollar Sunday

> Never doubt that a small group of thoughtful, committed citizens can change the world. Indeed, it is the only thing that ever has.
>
> —Margaret Mead

The first wave of expansion for our Impact100 model came as a result of the *People* magazine article. Inquiries came into my inbox with the intensity of a tsunami, as people from around the nation read this powerful story and hoped to replicate Impact100 in their communities. In hindsight, this reaction was predictable, and I probably should have seen it coming, but I had no idea.

After learning about Impact100 from the article in *People* magazine, Debbie Ritchie gathered a team of strong, generous women in her Pensacola Bay Area community and inspired them to join her in building a new kind of charitable organization—a new chapter of Impact100. She and the entire Impact100 Pensacola founding board spent quite a bit of time on the phone with me. They were hungry to learn all they could about how Impact100 works and why it was designed the way it was. As we spoke, their passion for making a difference was obvious, as was the determination of this team to do something special for their beloved community.

Understanding that the goal of every Impact100 chapter is to reach five hundred members, thereby giving away one grant in each of the five Focus Areas, they began speaking with women in their community and enticing them to join this movement. By the end of their first year, rather than launching with one-hundred-plus women, they had recruited 233 women and were poised to give away two grants of $116,500, making history as the first Impact100 chapter to give away two grants in their launch year.

First grants in Pensacola

The grants funded in 2004 were each transformational and sustainable. The first funded the creation of Pensacola Habitat for Humanity's Habitat ReStore, where home improvement and building supplies are sold to help fund Habitat homes in the region. Profits from the ReStore funded new homes for fourteen families in the first ten years after this grant was extended.

In addition, Impact100 Pensacola awarded $116,500 to the Good Samaritan Clinic, funding the creation of a medical clinic serving the low-income and uninsured residents of the community. The clinic is run by volunteer dentists, doctors, and nurses who treated over ten thousand patients in the first five years of operation.

In just four years, by 2008, Impact100 Pensacola Bay Area reached the goal of five hundred members, but did not stop there. They were giving away six grants by 2011, seven grants by 2012, and eight grants by 2013. In 2014, as Impact100 Pensacola celebrated its ten-year anniversary, they also celebrated a new and remarkable milestone:

giving away ten grants totaling $1,025,000 on a single day. It was a million-dollar Sunday—their first, but not their last. Beginning in 2018, they increased their giving to award eleven grants, and continue to give away eleven grants right through 2022.

Over the years, Impact100 Pensacola has given away a great deal of money that has changed many lives. One of my favorite grants from this chapter was in 2013 when $104,500 was awarded to a nonprofit called Independence for the Blind of West Florida. The grant was used to establish the Impact100 Windows to the World Technology Center, which provides both technology and transportation services for visually impaired residents.

The organization understood too well that their clients cannot take advantage of the training and services they offer if they are unable to get to their facility. Once at the facility, they also needed hands-on training and experience with technologies that their fully sighted friends often take for granted. Therefore, in addition to purchasing a safe, fuel-efficient vehicle that brings students to the facility, an Impact100 grant also equipped the learning center with new computers, iPhones, iPads, software, and assistive technology. The sustainable investment in establishing the center and purchasing the vehicle, along with robust technology assets, powerfully transformed the lives of visually impaired people in the region. This grant resulted in immediate, tangible benefits that will last well into the future.

Pensacola members: diverse and committed

We have Impact100 chapters in communities that are statistically wealthier than Pensacola, but no other Impact100 chapter comes close to Pensacola's membership numbers. There are many things that make Pensacola so special, and inclusivity is at the top of the list. The members of Impact100 Pensacola are as varied as the events that recruited them. Many of the women are seasoned philanthropists who give to Impact100 along with several other causes they find worthy. And many others have to sacrifice and save in order to fund their $1,000 membership dues.

One woman shared her story at the prompting of her friend, who is also a member: Back when she first heard about Impact100, she made a commitment to join. Fearful her husband would not agree, she dug up some jewelry she did not wear often and took it to a pawn shop. Between what she collected from the sale and her own savings, she could afford her first year's membership. By the following year, she still did not think her husband would approve, so again, she dug through her jewelry box and visited a jeweler. She was able to raise exactly what she needed. By the third year, her husband was convinced, and she no longer had to find inventive ways to fund her membership.

Like other Impact100 chapters, Pensacola quietly offers assistance to women who cannot afford a full membership. The expectation is that this help is temporary, until she can get back on her feet and make the full donation. That way, through private gifts, women receive the extra funds they need in order to join even when times are hardest.

Assembling a diverse, committed community of philanthropists is no easy feat, and in truth it cannot be accomplished without exceptional leadership. Since its founding, Impact100 Pensacola Bay Area has focused on building a leadership culture that is inclusive, consistent, and hardworking. Like most other Impact100 leadership teams, this is a working board of more than twenty highly capable women, each with an important role to play. The joke around the board table is that if they had to take a drink every time someone said, "This is a working board," they'd never get anything done because they'd be too drunk!

I have witnessed the annual meeting of the board, where outgoing members experience their final meeting while new members are welcomed to their new roles. The affection they have for each other and the organization is genuine. Tears fall from the eyes of those who feel sad to leave as well as from the eyes of those who feel so blessed to be chosen as an incoming leader.

While every board member works hard in her role, founding board member Belle Bear ensures they are intentional about staying true to the Impact100 model every step of the way. After being tested during their 2004 inaugural year with a hurricane devastating their community, they have remained relentless in their adherence to the Impact100 model. Our early conversations continued throughout the years, as board members often touched base when new heights were achieved and milestones passed.

Belle is the only member of the board who has served continuously since the beginning. A dynamic community advocate and philanthropist, her charismatic leadership carries great influence on the board and beyond. Between Belle and President Emeritus Debbie Ritchie, adherence to the model and keeping the culture strong by selecting the right leaders to the board has been paramount to the continued success of this chapter.

While they work hard, they also know how to have a really good time. Membership retention and recruitment is everyone's job—current and past board members included! Membership recruiting season offers a wide variety of activities for women to learn about Impact100 and join. Venues for recruiting range from beautiful Pensacola Beach to a local country club to a bus ride to a bar on the Florida-Alabama line to a fancy steakhouse and everything in between. All are welcome and there is something for everyone.

Increasing Your Impact

Pensacola, Florida, is a spectacularly beautiful community in Florida's panhandle. There are beautiful beaches, a vibrant downtown, and it is where the US Navy's elite pilots, the Blue Angels, call home. Demographically, this community does not have the wealth of many of our Impact100 communities, but it has the heart.

Pensacola did not set out to break records and grow beyond all expectations. Instead, they opened their hearts, minds, and checkbooks to help solve their community's most pressing problems. They held fast to the Impact100 model and have successfully avoided the so-called "mission creep" that can afflict nonprofits of every ilk. They have actively pursued members from every walk of life and attracted the best leaders to helm the organization—a deceptively simple formula that has been flawlessly executed.

9

Growing Pains

> It's like any investment. After all, you wouldn't put funds into
> stocks or bonds without understanding the potential return.
> Why wouldn't you do the same when investing in society?
>
> —Laura Arrillaga-Andreessen

The Impact100 model was born from the recognition that women continue to be faced with barriers to their involvement in philanthropy and community service. Although women's roles had evolved outside of the home and into the financial realm in the decades since the 1950s, the vehicles for women's leadership and philanthropic contribution had not kept pace. Anchored in my own experience, I was confident that our model would stack up—that the empowerment and collaboration of diverse women could ignite transformational change in local communities. Through this movement, more women would find their path to community service and philanthropy.

Several Impact100 chapters emerged in the wake of the *People* magazine article. As the article gained traction, the barriers I observed in Cincinnati, and the solution I designed through Impact100, seemed to resonate with women in communities near and far. These women were looking for a path into community engagement and philanthropy. They were looking for a new way to see the world and their role within it. Even if they could not fully articulate exactly what they'd needed or why, they had needed Impact100.

Tailor-made options for Impact100 chapters

There are so many unique aspects to the Impact100 model that draw women to it. Perhaps one of the most vital is that women design their own experience within their Impact100 chapter. If they choose to get involved as volunteers, there are plenty of opportunities that include all the training they will need to be effective. If they choose simply to donate, that is fine too. Regardless of their involvement level, it's one woman, one check, one vote.

Two chapters—one in Austin, Texas, and one in Pensacola, Florida—stayed closest to me during their initial founding. In each case, the founding president had read the magazine article and felt compelled to act. Each reached out to me and gathered her leadership team. I spent hours on the phone with the leaders from these two communities as they wrestled through their early growing pains, working through legal formation and creation, filing bylaws, and attracting local women to join their membership rosters.

Over the years, more and more Impact100 chapters started popping up. Some were a result of the *People* story, and others were due to the grassroots, word-of-mouth sharing of ideas. Friends, relatives, sorority sisters, and colleagues would spread the word about this new organization they were involved in. "The model is simple," they said. "You should build one in your community too." And so they did, and Impact100 continued to grow.

Facing a barrage of personal challenges

All this time that Impact100 was growing, my personal life had been imploding. As mentioned earlier, my marriage of sixteen years was ending. I relocated with our children to Northern Michigan to be closer to my father and stepmom as I started a new role at a new company and helped my kids adjust from a small private school to a larger public school.

During this season of my life, I remember seeing a chart used to estimate a person's stress level. It listed a slew of life events, rating them on the trauma and stress each carried. To determine your score, you were to tally each of the life events you were currently experiencing. My score during these years was off the charts.

- Separation and divorce after sixteen years of marriage: Check
- Young children with newly diagnosed learning disabilities: Check
- Selling your home: Check
- Leaving a strong network of friends: Check
- Financial disruption: Check
- Finding reliable day care: Check
- Moving to a new home, city, and state: Check, check, and check
- Finding a new job: Check
- Finding new schools for the kids: Check

- Comforting kids through all of these changes: Check
- Dating in my forties: Check
- Remarriage and blending two very different families into one: Check

During these incredibly challenging times, I would often take a walk to clear my thoughts or think through a problem. Typically following the same path, I would leave my office, cut through the parking lot and past the other businesses in the office park, and take a few laps around the sweeping cul-de-sac. Day after day, I walked at lunchtime, hoping the exercise, fresh air, and rhythmic cadence of my steps on the pavement would bring peace, clarity, and perspective to my mind.

Some days, I walked simply to escape, and I walked with music blasting through my headphones. Other days, I used the time to walk and talk, using my cell phone on the well-worn path to negotiate a deal or make a connection to a client, prospect, or vendor.

They say there are no atheists in a foxhole, and in my foxhole, I was desperate for hope and meaning amid the loss and heartbreak. Multiple research studies have validated the notion that an individual's faith or religious practice can confer positive mental health benefits, including easing the symptoms of stress, depression, and anxiety. My own personal experience has certainly reflected this idea as well. It was during this time of painful change in my life that I most actively explored my faith, reading the Bible and trying to find meaning in my struggles. I was looking for hope, comfort, and peace.

I had always believed the stories of the Bible in my youth. As an adult, I understood the basics of Christianity and considered myself to be a person of faith. But my life had gotten pretty busy and complicated, and I hadn't spent much time in church. So, in this time of renewed faith, my relationship with God was a deeply personal one.

On my most difficult days, as I walked off my stress and uncertainty, I also wrestled with my faith. I challenged God through a combination of prayer and venting—wondering why He was not more present in my life and the lives of those around me, more merciful to those who had faith in Him, or more prompt in His answers to our prayers. I also saw the way some people used their Christian faith as an excuse for bigotry and exclusion, and wondered why God didn't intervene. Was He even listening to me now? I knew I needed guidance, and if God had answers, then I needed to figure out how to hear them directly from the Big Guy Himself.

An everyday miracle growing in the sidewalk

It was on one of these walks, in the middle of another rambling monologue directed at God with my list of needs, wants, and complaints, that I looked down, and there it was. It stopped me dead in my tracks. Directly in the path that I had walked almost daily for months on end was a daisy. This was not just any daisy. The perfectly smooth blacktop had buckled in the road, and growing out of the cracked pavement was a perfect, single flower. A simple, beautiful daisy. Seeing it took my breath away, and I wondered what other gifts I had not seen. As I focused on my problems and my needs, I was missing the gifts and the little everyday miracles.

That daisy has become a symbol to me of God's grace and the miracles He provides every day if we would just take a moment to look for them. Recently, a dear friend gave me two necklaces, each with a perfect daisy preserved in clear resin on a lovely silver chain. I wear them often. Frequently, I select one of the two as a reminder to stay focused on the right things. On more difficult days, I wear them both, silently willing myself to see whole bouquets of daisies in the midst of challenge or difficulty.

These beautiful reminders work like a gratitude journal, reminding me to redirect my thoughts to what I am grateful for and away from the disappointments and difficulties. Keeping my attention on the bright spots, joyful moments, and everyday miracles has done wonders for me as I remain focused and search for the good in every situation.

Holding our first conference of Impact100 chapters

While my schedule seemed grueling enough on its own, I saw the need for bringing together the different chapters. I hosted the first Impact100 Conference in 2005. The idea was to bring together the three existing Impact100 chapters (Cincinnati, Pensacola, and Austin) to share best practices and build community as we nurtured and grew the movement. I chose Chicago for our conference because of its central location, the wide array of hotels, and the plethora of options for conference space.

The inaugural Impact100 Conference was a tremendous success. It was at this initial gathering that we determined a cadence and operating rhythm for future conferences. The idea was to meet once every few years with a different Impact100 chapter hosting the conference each time. While in Chicago, Impact Austin volunteered to host the next event. Conferences continued this way for many years, with the next chapter self-identifying as the new host during the closing hours of the current conference. Each successive conference was bigger and more robust than the one before as the Impact100 movement continued to thrive.

I carved out as much time as possible to serve and support the remarkable women who were building an Impact100 in their communities, but I know I let many of them down. I did not have the bandwidth to keep track of all the growth. I cheerfully helped where I could and gave as much encouragement as possible, hoping to equip these big-hearted women to successfully replicate the Impact100 model in their hometowns.

But as more women reached out, I found I was spread so thin, my help and guidance fell short of my own high standards, and I felt incredibly guilty and conflicted by the realities of my schedule and competing priorities.

Juggling full-time work with the needs of Impact100

During these years, I responded to the needs of Impact100 chapters and leaders as well as I could while working full-time and attending to the needs of my family. Coaching women as they brought Impact100 into their communities and their hearts has always been incredibly rewarding. If I could have at that time, I would have happily devoted all of my working hours to supporting the Impact100 community—but that wasn't financially feasible.

So I did as much as I could while juggling a full-time career, three kids, two golden retrievers, and the chaos that accompanies each. But I kept wrestling with the notion of making Impact100 my full-time work. It was clear that the Impact100 community needed more than just my spare time, but I simply couldn't make the math work.

I read countless books and consulted with business coaches, financial advisors, and life coaches, but the results all pointed to the same solution: The best way to make working for the benefit of Impact100 chapters around the globe a paying job was to charge each chapter a fee to engage with me and use the Impact100 model.

This was out of the question for a variety of reasons, not the least of which is that the Impact100 model itself was designed to pass 100 percent of the members' annual donations through to the local community in significant grants. Insisting on being funded by the chapters would set up a system that worked against the very model it was designed to support.

Launching my for-profit consultancy

In 2013, I launched Generosity Matters, a for-profit consultancy designed to help families, communities, and organizations cultivate a culture of generosity. Although not perfect, this was the best solution I could devise. Through Generosity Matters, I repurposed much of the work I gave to Impact100 chapters free of charge and connected with paying clients to share this knowledge. I worked with organizations both large and small as they wrestled with the notion of empowering employees to act generously with each other and with their clients, vendors, and communities. I also worked with high-net-worth families who sought to responsibly pass their values (and valuables) on to future generations.

Through Generosity Matters, I addressed community groups and families to unpack the notion that when we give, we benefit ourselves, our families, and our workplaces in powerful and often unexpected ways. I encouraged generosity and promoted the idea that everyone had something to give; giving has a strong multiplier effect, and we need not wait a moment to give generously. My Impact100 work was still a side gig, but I often found Impact100 members attending talks I gave when engaged as a Generosity

Matters consultant. Many of the examples I spoke of were born from my Impact100 experience.

At the time, I didn't comprehend the impact of my inability to fully support Impact100 chapters. What I recognize now is that, left to their own devices, these courageous leaders did the best they could to implement the Impact100 model. In some cases, not understanding the importance of a large and diverse board made growth and sustainability a more significant challenge than it might have been otherwise. Some leaders did not fully understand aspects of the Impact100 model and sometimes dismissed ideas as not right for a specific community.

In every case, regardless of how they interpreted the Impact100 process, these hardworking and committed leaders did everything they could to launch, nurture, and grow Impact100 successfully. The Impact100 movement was spreading, growing pains and all.

Increasing Your Impact

Growing pains can happen for a variety of reasons. Although this conversation is centered on the growth of the movement and the role of Impact100 Global, individual chapters also experience growing pains of their own. Some can be anticipated and addressed early, while others tend to quietly creep in almost without notice. Although Impact100 Global does not presently have the capacity to proactively reach out to ease the pains that arise, our plan is to do just that. It will be a game-changer for our chapters and the communities they serve.

As the Impact100 movement grows, something unexpected has started to happen. Members of local Impact100 chapters are reaching out to me at Impact100 Global to give and support our work. Generous women have given personally, and chapters have given as well. Although I cannot imagine a time where a fixed donation is mandated, I do see that the Impact100 movement is strongest when we support each other so that all chapters have access to the training and resources needed to reach their highest potential.

10

Global Movement

> Trust yourself. Create the kind of self that you will be happy to live with all of your life. Make the most of yourself by fanning the tiny, inner sparks of possibility into flames of achievement.
>
> —Golda Meir

While much of Impact100 was centered in the United States and grew by word of mouth, with help from local and national media coverage here and there, the spread of Impact100 outside the United States happened unexpectedly.

Early in 2011, the Australian government had a well-developed strategy to better understand best practices for increasing philanthropic support, particularly to arts organizations. About this time, the Fundraising Institute of Australia Perpetual Scholarship awarded James Boyd, West Australian manager of Artsupport Australia, an office of the Australia Council for the Arts, a grant to study and assess American funding solutions with a grassroots component.

This work brought him to the United States, where he researched a variety of collective giving models and met with and interviewed community foundations and other community-focused givers. In due time, he completed a comprehensive report and spoke at a number of national conferences about his research.

Soon after this project deadline, James met up with a friend over a morning coffee, and she asked about his project. James shared stories from his trip to the United States and shared some of the things he learned during this work. She asked which of the giving models he had researched held the most promise, and he told her about Impact100. He explained how powerful and efficient Impact100 was and shared stories from his time with various chapters.

Intrigued, his friend asked James what he was going to do now. He responded that the work was completed and his report was already submitted, so he was finished. She asked, again, what he would do about Impact100. Again, he said that he had already submitted the report. Exasperated, she practically shouted: "James, why don't we start an Impact100 chapter here in Perth?" And so it began.

Launching Impact100 in Australia

Impact100 WA (Western Australia) launched in May of 2012. James became an honorary Australian ambassador for collective giving and Impact100. He helped to foster chapters in Melbourne, South Australia, Sydney, Queensland, North Sydney, Fremantle, and Tasmania. He convenes national conferences in Australia to celebrate successes, encourage growth of collective giving generally and Impact100 specifically, and share best practices. Although I have happily participated virtually, it will be a joy to join them in person one day.

In the Land Down Under, all but the Queensland chapter of

Impact100 are gender neutral, with men and women serving and leading together. People often ask me why the Australian chapters invite men, whereas most Impact100 chapters, globally, are for women. The answer boils down to cultural context and objectives. When I originally created Impact100 in America, I was focused on the disparity between men and women when it came to giving. My goal was to empower women to give with the same confidence and freedom as their male counterparts.

The cultural issues surrounding philanthropy in Australia are entirely different. Philanthropy was not something openly discussed by Australians. Those who did give most often did so quietly and privately. These cultural differences made the Impact100 model appealing to Australians of all genders as a fully transparent process where each member has an equal voice. Both men and women would benefit from the Impact100 model equally, as their barriers to philanthropy were more nationwide than they were gender specific.

Building local Impact100 communities helped educate members about the best solutions available and how to vet and assess the efficacy of each funding proposal. The model helped members to see themselves as philanthropists and as a part of the solution to their community's most pressing problems.

As the Impact100 model spreads around the globe, I look forward to working alongside brilliant colleagues and friends like James and others to design culturally aligned practices that meet the needs of each nation with its unique social makeup and attitudes toward philanthropy.

First conference of Impact100 Global

Impact100's path to global visibility wasn't entirely linear. While the *People* article had certainly raised the organization's profile and new

Impact100 chapters were being rolled out in far-flung places like Australia, tried-and-true conferences still continued to be a valuable community-building tool.

The problem was, they were also a significant undertaking for our unpaid volunteers and me. It was becoming too much to successfully execute a significant conference while running an Impact100 chapter at the same time. In 2014, I reimagined the Impact100 Conference concept with the understanding that the movement had outgrown our grassroots approach to convening.

After discussions with Impact100 leaders, we targeted October of 2016 as the first Impact100 Global Conference hosted by all five of the Impact100 chapters in Florida. I was to co-host, and in 2015, we filed the necessary paperwork to begin offering conferences and other resources to Impact100 chapters through the Impact100 Global Advisory Council—Impact100 Global, for short.

Impact100 Global serves two related but separate audiences: start-up chapters and existing chapters. The organization's mission is to nurture, support, and encourage Impact100 start-up chapters from concept to launch and initial grantmaking to ensure they begin on solid footing with tools for success.

At the same time, Impact100 Global seeks to proactively support existing Impact100 chapters through each stage of growth, including leadership succession, community partnerships, recruitment and retention, nonprofit development and relations, and board development and administration.

The original mission statement for Impact100 Global was:

The mission of Impact100 Global Advisory Council is to encourage collaboration and sharing of best practices among Impact100 groups to allow for continued growth and sustainability of Impact100 around the world. We will create world-class strategic philanthropy and transform communities with significant grants while we equip individuals to become effective philanthropists and guide them to amplify their success for positive change.

We would later revise and shorten the statement to read:

Impact100 is a collective force for good; uniting and empowering women to give together, creating transformational impact, locally and globally.

The model is simple, but execution can be tricky

Ultimately, it was clear then, as it is now, that although Impact100 is a powerfully simple model, executing it well is not easy. Existing chapters needed support in order to reach their highest potential. Communities hoping to begin a new Impact100 chapter needed resources and tools to launch well and succeed in their goal of transforming their local community.

For existing Impact100 chapters, the demand for information, assistance, and resources was continuous. Chapters are typically led by a fully volunteer team. By design, the leadership team is meant to turn over regularly, meaning there are always new leaders stepping up as trained leaders step away. Women were passionate about the work but needed education to successfully continue the work their predecessors began.

Often, the institutional knowledge the chapter was founded upon was not well-documented and risked getting lost in translation. As an organization grew and matured, each had growing pains as they managed a larger membership roster and worked to ensure that quality nonprofit applications flowed continuously.

New Impact100 chapters needed different resources. First, they needed to fully understand the elements of the Impact100 model and why it works the way it does. From there, they would start to assemble a diverse team of high-capacity women with the myriad skills needed to launch a successful chapter. These leaders needed to understand the technicalities of filing for their nonprofit status, building a website, opening bank accounts, and determining their grant process and calendar.

Each start-up chapter tends to move at its own pace. Some leadership teams take their time, carefully introducing the concept and adding leaders with care and conviction. Others race through the start-up process, eager to get going and distribute the newly gathered funding quickly and efficiently. One way is not better than another. The timeline works best when the leadership team is confident in the path forward and as each step falls into place.

As I write this, 2022—our twenty-first-anniversary year—is drawing to a close, and Impact100 has revolutionized philanthropy as a global organization delivering local impact all over the world. The success of this women's collective giving model is undeniable. By the end of 2022, our more than thirty thousand members helped us exceed $123 million in grantmaking over the course of our twenty-one-year history. We firmly believe in the collaboration and empowerment of diverse women to lead transformational change in their communities.

Today, we have more than sixty-five active Impact100 chapters and almost fifty communities eager to launch an Impact100 chapter in cities around the world. But back in 2015, I couldn't see that future. Impact100 was growing faster than we could keep up with and experiencing growing pains we weren't yet built to tackle. The pull to devote more time to the Impact100 movement was powerful. I am grateful to have some good friends and mentors who helped me imagine what could be possible and explore potential funding models to support the Impact100 movement and allow me to devote my full attention to the movement I had launched so many years ago.

This was anything but easy. In 2015, Rick and I celebrated our tenth wedding anniversary as the oldest of our five kids, Stephen, was completing college; the next three, Alex, Brooke, and Hailey, were in college; and our youngest, Jake, was poised to begin his college journey in two short years. These were busy and expensive times—times when I needed a paycheck more than ever, times that demanded practical solutions, not daydreams of working full-time for a nonprofit without an established funding source or donor base.

One meeting changes everything

In May of 2016, my life and the trajectory of Impact100 changed drastically. Vice president and "chief disrupter" of the Morgridge Family Foundation (MFF), Carrie Morgridge, reached out through my Generosity Matters website to request a Zoom meeting. She had recently spoken at the annual meeting of Impact the Palm Beaches. She explained that she was a fan of Impact100 and wanted to learn more. Her "deputy disrupter," John Farnam, joined us on the call.

After introductions and a few pleasantries, Carrie cut right to the chase by asking how I received compensation for my work with Impact100. I chuckled a bit, in part because this very question had been on my mind for years—I worked a day job full-time in order to offer my work supporting Impact100 chapters and leaders around the globe for free. I explained that my work with Generosity Matters

INVITATION TO IMPACT

paid the bills and that my work with Impact100 was pro bono. I watched her face fall as I spoke, and she remarked that my lack of sustainability did not bode well for the future of Impact100.

Although I knew she was right, I had mentally wrestled with every conceivable revenue plan, and none aligned with the notion that Impact100 chapters were designed to be pass-through foundations, giving away 100 percent of their members' contributions in sizable grants to their local community. They did not have excess funds to pay me, and I didn't want them to sacrifice the power of the Impact100 model to receive much-needed funding. I smiled weakly while explaining this dilemma.

Not discouraged, perhaps even a bit energized, Carrie and John got creative and suggested various ways to raise the start-up capital and build a sustainable infrastructure for the Impact100 movement. Unfortunately, these solutions did not align with the premise of Impact100, and I had the burden of eliminating each potential funding source. We ended our first meeting committed to reconnecting in a couple of weeks.

Within a week, Carrie called again. She said that she had fact-checked my objections from the last call and agreed they would not be suitable avenues for growth. In the absence of a firm plan, she volunteered to serve on our board and to fund Impact100 Global with a three-year commitment that would not only provide a salary for me, but would also fund a new website and other marketing expenses, too.

This very moment was another turning point in my life, and one I will never forget. I told her that her gift was validation of my work and would allow us the foundation to build long-term sustainability for Impact100. This gift allowed me to fully devote my time and energy to supporting the Impact100 movement. It allowed us to dream big and begin building the kind of resources Impact100 chapters and leaders have needed for years.

Tweaking and again expanding the Impact100 model

This was only the beginning. Carrie immersed herself in the Impact100 community. She has been not only financially generous to our community, but she has also opened doors for us and introduced me to so many people in her network. She spoke at our 2016 Global Conference, and through MFF she funded grants to allow every Impact100 chapter around the globe to offer a 50 percent membership match for two women who otherwise couldn't afford to join. She then funded our inaugural Young Philanthropist Program (YPP) grants, offering each chapter the ability to nurture one or two young women in their community as Impact100 members.

YPP is a multiyear commitment designed to instill in eligible and interested young women the habit of financial budgeting for charitable giving as well as time management to allow volunteer time each year. Our YPP contribution toward the young philanthropists' $1,000 membership decreased each year until the fourth year, when each young woman paid her membership in full.

For several years, Carrie held the unique title as the *only* member of *every* Impact100 chapter around the globe. Her generosity is tangible to each Impact100 chapter: Her membership provides a genuine connection to communities and leaders around the world as she, with the help of the MFF team, joyfully casts her vote for grant recipients in each Impact100 chapter.

Early in 2020, before the realities of the COVID-19 pandemic hit, I made my first trip to visit several chapters in Australia with

Carrie and her team. We spent a great deal of time with leaders from Impact100 chapters in Melbourne, South Australia, Sydney, North Sydney, and—where it all began—with James Boyd from Perth. This trip allowed me to meet with grant recipients as well as many of the Impact100 members in Australia. I was then able to join them in New Zealand where I was introduced to a dynamic friend of Carrie's who was so inspired, she became the founding president of our first New Zealand chapter, Impact100 Wakatipu.

Carrie's bold and generous support has been a game-changer for the work of Impact100 Global. As our lead funder and "chief cheerleader," Carrie and MFF modeled the idea that in order for this global movement to thrive, we needed sustainable infrastructure.

What I have come to understand is when people hear about Impact100, the most common reaction is to want to join an existing chapter or launch a new chapter in their local area. It is this very reaction that has fueled the growth of the Impact100 movement around the globe. In fact, as I write this, the number of communities looking to begin a new Impact100 chapter is increasing almost weekly. In addition, we are seeing existing Impact100 chapters increasing their membership rolls as well. This is outstanding news especially as we consider the impact of mobilizing more philanthropists around the globe to solve our most pressing problems by awarding sizable grants to local nonprofits.

One aspect of Impact100 chapter growth that I am most proud of is the fact that when an Impact100 chapter gets launched in a new community, we do not take the existing pie of philanthropic giving and divide it differently so Impact100 gets a piece of it at the expense of other organizations. Instead, Impact100 grows the pie of philanthropic giving by engaging new donors and involving people who previously didn't see their role in community philanthropy.

Experienced philanthropists most often add Impact100 to their portfolio of giving rather than substituting it for another giving priority.

Starting new and strengthening existing Impact100 chapters remains a top priority

As Impact100 chapters grow and new Impact100 chapters are launched, the demand for resources and training provided by Impact100 Global increases exponentially. Impact100 Global leverages our decades of experience working with this unique collective giving model to help effectively launch new Impact100 chapters and lift existing chapters to their highest potential. We do this through customized coaching, robust training, and effective tools designed to ensure the success and sustainability of Impact100 chapters well into the future.

Fortunately, there are also people and organizations who recognize the vital role that Impact100 Global plays in ensuring the continued strength and longevity of the Impact100 movement and generously support our work. In the same way that a member's $1,000 donation to an Impact100 chapter is multiplied to become a $100,000 grant as others join, donations to Impact100 Global are multiplied to benefit every single chapter around the globe.

It may surprise you to know that I have found it difficult, at times, to ask for donations to benefit Impact100 Global. Although I have spent a great deal of my adult life encouraging generosity and inviting people to donate to myriad causes and organizations, this felt different somehow. I suppose it felt more personal.

I recognized the mental block and utilized a strategy I have so often coached others to employ. I thought through the tactical and philosophical reasons why I give and why funding is so urgently needed. Once I did that, I was able to separate my personal connection and instead focus on the mission of the organization. If we want Impact100 to thrive into the future, Impact100 Global needs to be sustainable.

> ## Increasing Your Impact
>
> For most of the more than twenty-year history of Impact100, I have worked without pay to serve Impact100 leadership and support Impact100 chapters around the world. This is not a "humble brag" about my work ethic or sacrifice for the good of the movement. Rather, it is a conviction that this practice is not sustainable, and it does not serve the Impact100 movement well.
>
> Achieving a sustainable level of funding to enable fairly compensated professionals to execute the mission of Impact100 Global through education, coaching, and resources is vital. Anything less will jeopardize the viability of the Impact100 movement.

11

The Company You Keep

> Differences can be a strength.
>
> —Condoleezza Rice

As we discovered in growing the global Impact100 community, cultivating the right people to walk alongside you in life does far more than build strength in your organization—it can build strength in your own character. It's been said that we are the sum of the people we spend the most time with. I believe this to be true. When we spend time with people who are well-read, we learn. Spending time with people who eat well and live a healthy lifestyle will encourage us to do the same.

A great source of strength and hope for me is my family. I am grateful to find my family members truly inspiring and thoughtful. Beginning with my dad and grandparents and continuing now with my husband, kids, sisters, and in-laws, spending time with family always teaches me something important. But I have discovered that while my family might form the cornerstone of my inner circle, for everyone's health and success, my family can't be the only people I allow into that circle. Fortunately, I have also been blessed with close friends who elevate my thoughts and expand my worldview, often sharing book recommendations or talking about things that matter as we hunt shells, rocks, or thrift store bargains together.

For many years, I have been part of a Friday morning CEO group that I've found to be particularly beneficial. We began as a sort of "mastermind" group for CEOs—all women—leading distinctly different organizations. This group has evolved into so much more. Sure, we still share our business challenges and successes, but we also work through personal triumphs and disappointments. The group began as a monthly in-person meeting. Like so much else, when we faced the pandemic, we quickly shifted to meeting virtually.

The most powerful iteration for this group was the pivot from meeting one Friday a month to meeting every Friday. Triggered by the quickly shifting sands of work, home, and health, we each had too much happening each week to delay conversations for weeks. This community of women has provided wisdom, compassion, and sound guidance along with prayer and heartfelt friendship. Years of consistently being vulnerable and transparent together and holding each other accountable has built a powerful and lasting connection.

Choose wisely what you let into your life

Give yourself permission to curate your life by intentionally spending time with people who help you to be the best version of yourself. You do not need to be in the same neighborhood or workplace to spend time with people who matter to you. Technology allows regular communication with family, friends, colleagues, and others who aren't even in the same time zone. Scheduling weekly phone or Zoom calls keeps you connected to loved ones regardless of their geography.

You can also surround yourself with people you admire simply by reading their books and listening to their podcasts or TED talks. You have the ability to determine what news you take in and at what time of day. Being intentional about what input you allow into your mind can be a real game-changer. Today, we live in a never-ending news cycle. Choose wisely, then design your days and weeks to give you what you need in the form of both information and inspiration.

While being choosy about the people and ideas in which you invest your time and attention can reap enormous benefits both personally and professionally, a diversity of thought is essential for ensuring that you maintain a well-rounded perspective—especially for those working in the nonprofit space. When selecting your sources of input and inspiration, do not limit yourself to business books and resources within your industry or concentration. New ideas often come from unexpected places.

Be sure to read and learn from those outside your field. The information you learn from outside your area of expertise, when coupled with your personal work and industry experience, may lead to the breakthrough thinking you have been searching for. This is a habit I developed long ago, and it has not only made my life far more interesting, but it has proven to be an accessible way to reach better decisions.

Diverse on purpose

The Impact100 model is designed to be diverse and inclusive. Starting with the founding leadership team, being intentional about recruiting a diverse pool of talented leaders is a key success measure and

Impact100 model best practice. We may be tempted to believe that diversity will come later or that diversity will arise organically as the word of our work spreads. Believing these myths will only perpetuate the status quo.

Diversity must be a priority. Creating a diverse and inclusive organization does not happen without consistent attention. It is vital to attract and retain leaders and members who appropriately represent the community that an Impact100 chapter serves. That means mirroring the community with regard to ethnicity, faith, marital status, age, profession, and sexual orientation. It means drawing from every part of town, every possible demographic, and with newcomers to the community serving alongside women whose families have lived there for generations.

Most Impact100 chapters include diversity and inclusion as a priority, but Impact100 St. Lucie, Florida, brings this commitment to the next level. As founding president Debbie Butler says, "Without diversity among our members, how could we possibly be leaders in our community to bring about change? By having women from all walks of life, we are better equipped to serve our community. A diverse group of women makes for greater impact—if we were all from the same background or walk of life, we would not be able to think outside the box."

Debbie didn't just invite diverse women to serve on her board, she also made certain they were visible and asked them to take an active role in telling the story of Impact100 and inviting women to join. Giving women a face and a voice, along with a vital role to play on the team, increases connection. Many of the women Debbie recruited to join her as members were friends or business connections, but not all. Debbie always kept a small Impact100 brochure with her. She was known to hand them out to strangers in line at the store or at community events. Her broad smile and insistence they become a part of the Impact100 movement made her difficult to refuse.

Even if they did not ultimately join her, Debbie was happy knowing that they would know about Impact100 and possibly encourage a nonprofit to apply. Plus, there was always next year. Looking at her results, making diversity a priority works: Almost 40 percent of the Impact100 St. Lucie founding members are women of color, which closely mirrors the community demographics.

Of course, there are many Impact100 chapters focused on cultivating a diverse community where all are included and welcome. Notably, Impact100 DC, Impact100 Metro Detroit, Impact100 Houston, and Impact100 Seattle come to mind as they intentionally build diverse teams where all are included. Impact100 Pensacola Bay Area has been so intentionally inclusive that its more than 1,100 members come from every conceivable background and demographic. Each Impact100 community works toward this ideal with intention and understanding. It is an ever-evolving goal, and we still have much more to do.

When we consider diversity, equity, and inclusion, Impact100 does not just look within, but also without. Our grant application and assessment protocols also incorporate these values. One of the questions we ask a nonprofit applying for a grant addresses representation. Specifically, we consider how well the demographics of their board and senior staff reflect the community they serve. Because representation and diversity of thought are the most effective tools we have in problem-solving for our communities, the relationship between the demographics of the nonprofit's leadership and the demographics of its community is an essential data point in our review and application process.

INVITATION TO IMPACT

The promise of Impact100

Impact100 is grounded in the belief that we are stronger together. We believe in the collaboration and empowerment of diverse women to ignite transformational change in our communities. Our voice is stronger, our decisions are more informed, and our impact is amplified when we bring together all people, each with an equal say in the outcome.

As a collective-giving group, we celebrate these principles in all that we do. Both locally and globally, every Impact100 chapter aspires to reflect the communities we serve by attracting members representing every zip code, age bracket, race, ethnic group, sexual orientation, marital status, and experience. Together, we fund powerful, transformational solutions to the most pressing problems facing our communities, but we do not stop there. We also serve as connectors by bringing the needs of our local nonprofits to the people who have the resources to help. We lift and celebrate the local leaders and organizations who are working diligently to make a powerful difference in the world.

The persistent inequities across our country and the world underscore our urgent need to address and alleviate racial, ethnic, and other tensions and to promote diversity within our communities. We know that diversity is good for our communities, our Impact100 chapters, our economy, and our own lives. The data is clear: Organizations with diverse teams perform better. We recognize that diversity and inclusion are multifaceted issues and that we need to tackle these subjects holistically to better engage and support all underrepresented groups. We know change does not happen overnight and will only come through intentional action and commitment.

With this in mind, on July 1, 2020, I signed the CEO Action for Diversity & Inclusion™ pledge, committing myself and Impact100

Global to advance diversity and inclusion in our workplaces, communities, and society. This community of more than a thousand business leaders representing every industry and sector is the largest CEO-driven commitment of its kind.

The CEO Action for Diversity & Inclusion™ initiative aims to rally community leaders to advance diversity and inclusion by working collectively across organizations and sectors. For Impact100 Global, the CEO Action Pledge is an important next step in cultivating an environment that supports open and honest dialogue on the complex issues of diversity and inclusion. The key commitment here is to act. Signatories of the pledge commit to taking action to advance diversity and inclusion in our organizations.

The feeling of belonging

Although representation is a great starting point for a new Impact100 chapter, cultivating a true sense of belonging within an Impact100 chapter is a vital aspect of our work. It's a powerful emotion to feel like you belong. It's a feeling that can unite whole nations—or divide them. And if nurtured with care and awareness, a sense of belonging can become the invisible thread that binds the members of your organization into a cohesive community, more powerful together than they ever had hope of being individually.

Growing up watching my grandmother host events in her home provided tangible clues about how to intentionally build a sense of belonging. The details—greeting people one at a time and truly connecting, offering food or drink that accommodates cultural and medical dietary restrictions, and being respectful of time and drawing everyone into the conversation—all help to create a sense of shared purpose and belonging.

Every Impact100 chapter works to make each member feel this way, even if we use more corporate language than my grandmother might have, such as "member engagement" or "member retention."

As a woman, I have been in the position of being the *only* woman on a board or leadership team. In the past, my decision to accept the role has been guided partly by my sense of belonging in the organization. My assessment of whether I am being included because of my expertise and skill set or because they would like a token woman on the team is what determines my response when asked to participate. I vividly remember being invited to serve on a board of an organization I had admired. The board chair invited me for coffee to discuss the board role. He shared that he was asking me to serve because they had received survey feedback that they were "out of touch" with their current board, made up of all men who were notably also all white and all about the same age. He went on to say that I was a good candidate, because my banking background assured him I would "think like a businessman" and not "a housewife." Needless to say, we didn't make it through coffee before I declined the offer. Clearly, this was not the kind of culture where I felt I would belong.

Diversity, equity, and inclusion

> Diversity is being invited to the party. Inclusion is being asked to dance. Belonging is being part of the party planning.
>
> —Vernā Myers (adapted)

The quote above is the North Star we use as we lead the Impact100 community through this important work. When we launched the new Impact100 Diversity, Equity, and Inclusion Committee in 2020, we hoped to provide tangible ways to assess and understand what it means to belong and how that sense of feeling a part of an Impact100 community can determine the success of our work.

To demonstrate the importance of this work, I serve as co-chair of this committee along with Amy Bouque, former president of Impact100 Metro Detroit. Amy's roles in HR for both Ally Financial and Kelly Services make her a seasoned professional in this work. She has been an invaluable asset to every facet of our DEI efforts. We have a long way to go in this area, but keeping the conversation top of mind and taking action to keep progressing on the journey is what we ask of our leaders, members, and ourselves. This is not a stand-alone committee or flavor-of-the-month temporary priority. This work is woven into the very fabric of all we do at Impact100.

After identifying the three pillars of engagement for our DEI work, we invited Impact100 members from around the globe to join our newly established Impact100 Global DEI Committee. Those pillars are Listen, Link Arms, and Lead.

Knowing we had a great deal to learn, an educational component was woven into each of our pillars. Several Impact100 chapters followed suit and created DEI initiatives at the local level. We began with implicit bias training and created additional curriculum in Impact Manager, our online module-based training system.

In our Community Forum, we also shared access to the resources available to CEO Pledge signatories. We incorporated several DEI-related sessions and keynotes into our 2021 Impact100 Global Conference and held independent training sessions, discussion groups, and open forum conversations where we shared best practices and additional resources.

Equity vs. Equality

As we were launching the Impact100 Global DEI Committee, we wrestled a bit with semantics. Using the right language in the proper context was important. One of the concepts we debated was equality versus equity. Although both have a place, we landed on equity over equality for our work. To understand why, consider this example:

Scenario 1: I have three children, ages eighteen, twenty-three, and twenty-seven, whom I love equally. In my estate planning documents, I advise my planning attorney to treat them equally. The day after I execute those documents, I am hit by a bus. My entire estate is worth $150,000. When divided equally among my three heirs, each child receives $50,000. Seems fair, doesn't it?

Scenario 2: The exact same conditions as the example above—except this time, I ask my estate planning attorney to treat my children equitably. After being hit by the same bus, and having a total estate of $150,000, here is what happens. Before my death, I fully paid for child 1's and 2's college education so they would graduate without any student loans. Had I survived, I would have paid the third child's tuition as well. In order to be equitable, my estate would first cover (or set aside funds) for child number 3's education before dividing the balance of the estate into three equal pieces.

In the first scenario, child number 3 would end up with a smaller portion of my estate simply because she hadn't been old enough to get a college degree.

Likewise, making the Impact100 membership and application experiences equitable will result in better outcomes. For example, in order to attract a broader economic and ethnic mix of members, several chapters have created a scholarship program that both augments a member's donation in order to reach the $1,000 fee if they are experiencing an economic hardship, and builds a cohort of scholarship recipients so these new members have a community within a community as they join Impact100. I recently heard from a chapter that, until a new board member spoke up, had given no consideration as to whether the monthly meeting time and place was on an accessible bus line. Our biggest event, the Annual Awards Celebration, has been an event that members pay to attend. Beginning with our inaugural meeting, we have offered an opportunity for members who find this charge financially inaccessible to confidentially have the fee covered, no questions asked. It is not always the easiest path, but it is the most inclusive.

> ## Increasing Your Impact
>
> The Chinese philosopher Lao Tzu is quoted as saying, "When I let go of who I am, I become what I might be."[11] So often we define ourselves in a certain way, or worse, we allow others to define us. This quote reminds me that it is ultimately our choice to decide what we might be. Our future selves can be more open, thoughtful, and kind. We could be the type of leader we admire or entrepreneur we dream to be.
>
> Surrounding ourselves with people who make us kinder, smarter, and more joyful is an important part of self-care and personal growth. Seeking out divergent views and lived experiences while staying open to learning new things often brings new understanding of perspectives outside our own. It enriches us personally and helps us to grow in myriad ways.

---

11 John Heider, *The Tao of Leadership: Lao Tzu's* Tao Te Ching *Adapted for a New Age* (Atlanta: Green Dragon Books, 2005).

12

When Disaster Strikes

The great gift of human beings is that we have the power of empathy.

—Meryl Streep

By late 2017, it was clear that having family close by would be a benefit to Rick's parents, Bob and Carlie, who lived on the west coast of Florida. Meanwhile, Rick and I found ourselves as empty nesters and our Michigan family home sat quiet, with just the two of us most of the time, as our children were largely launched and we had lost the second of our beloved golden retrievers, Shadow and Sunny. Since we both work remotely, nothing was preventing us from spending more time in the Sunshine State with this couple we love so much.

The decision made, we headed south and moved into a rented house close to Carlie and Bob. The move was a win-win-win for everyone. We were not only close to Rick's parents, but we were also close to dear friends in Sarasota, and close to the beach. In time, both my sister Tina and my dearest friend from college, Lisa, and her husband, Tony, moved to the area as well. Any hesitation I had felt about leaving Michigan quickly dissipated.

Our family grew by one soon after the move when we gratefully adopted a little Yorkie-mix puppy from a local rescue. We named her Gracie, and she quickly became a vital part of our family. A small dog was something new for us, as all of our previous dogs had been large. Although she was a challenge to housebreak, her sweet disposition and desire to be by our side in every activity made her not-so-occasional potty accidents a minor issue. She eventually caught on, of course, and also became a fan of paddleboarding, swimming, boating, and beach walking. Most days, she sits in my office as I work, often making a cameo on video calls.

The beauty of sea glass

Relocating to Florida meant the beach was always nearby. Walking the beach continues to provide great joy, inspiration, and peace. In addition to shells, I also collect sea glass and beach glass. For the uninitiated—sea glass comes from saltwater, and beach glass comes from freshwater. In fact, these kinds of glass aren't natural products at all. They get their start as some kind of refuse—a glass vase or bowl or cup or bottle—which somehow finds its way into our waters.

When I picture how beach glass is made, I love to imagine a shipwreck or a late-night party on the beach where a couple of bottles of someone's favorite beverage are somehow swept away by the high tide. These bottles are broken into shards with sharp edges and are clearly no longer what they once were. But by the time beach glass reappears on the shore, it's been smoothed and beautifully frosted by its ordeal. Those painful jagged edges are gone, and in their place is something remarkable, something precious and rare to hold in your hand or carry in your pocket so you will always remember this transformation.

I see this beach glass as a reflection not only of our lives but of the lives of those we serve when we give back. We all start off a certain way, and we believe that's who we are. And then life happens. We may experience tragedy, and whether it's an economic problem, a health problem, or a relational problem, it happens. But who we are today is better because of the struggle; what happens to that glass is, as it gets tossed and turned on the waves and the rocks and the rough sand, it becomes something more. We bring our life experiences to our generosity, to our philanthropy, and we better understand who needs us and who has the right solutions for our community's most pressing problems. And we understand that there are things we can do and others that we must do.

To me, beach glass is all about transformation. It's about accepting who we are and understanding that while failure and heartbreak might be disappointing and difficult, it's not permanent. Those of us who can figure out how to rise above those circumstances will become better and can shine the light for others who are in the midst of the difficult times, because we know what we would have wanted when we walked that same path.

That degree of empathy and understanding can only come through personal experience. It's the difference between having book knowledge of what someone might be facing versus having faced a similar circumstance, be it not knowing how to pay all the bills or holding the hand of a loved one who is struggling through an illness without a cure. We start to understand and heal ourselves when our personal struggles carve out a deeper level of compassion for others. We were brought into these circumstances not only for the experience of loss but for what that will strengthen and empower us to do next.

When we think back on our own lives, we will find that there are certain events that have shaped who we are. Some of these events are major milestones like graduations, weddings, moving to a new city, or having a baby. In other cases, the events may not be surrounded by ceremony, planning, or celebration. For example, that day you tried out for the team, received a speeding ticket, or lost a school election. In these moments, our values, our priorities, and our true essence are revealed. These moments can accelerate or completely change the trajectory of our lives.

So, as we think back on those times, we need to consider what we can do with our experience and with those rough edges, because only through the lens of those circumstances can we truly relate to people who are in need and assess the solutions offered by the community organizations seeking to serve them.

Defining moments show what we're about

Defining moments don't just shape our lives; they also define the organizations we champion. In his book *Start with Why: How Great Leaders Inspire Everyone to Take Action*, Simon Sinek explains that culture and employee morale are closely tied to the many defining moments leaders create. Actions and decisions that echo and reinforce the company's stated core values help to strengthen company culture, while behaviors of leaders in conflict with the organization's core values undermine the organization's work. Among Impact100 organizations, I have heard many stories of defining moments, and I wish I could share them all. Instead, I would like to include two, in hopes they will inspire.

Hurricane in Pensacola

The first story takes place back in September of 2004. When Impact100 Pensacola Bay Area was about to announce their inaugural list of five nonprofit finalists, Hurricane Ivan struck the region with catastrophic force. This storm resulted in significant damage and loss of lives in Pensacola and the surrounding area.

As you might imagine, the community was devastated. When people realized that Impact100 had $233,000 set aside for local grantmaking, the founding board received a great deal of pressure to redirect those funds. They were asked to forego the five finalist organizations (as they had been selected but not yet made public) and instead deploy those much-needed funds directly to hurricane relief. Understand that this storm had catastrophically affected many members of Impact100 Pensacola, including those on the founding board. This was a difficult decision.

Ultimately, the chapter stayed true to the original plan. They understood that hurricane relief would come from organizations skilled at this sort of assistance. They realized they had an obligation to fulfill the commitment they made when they collected membership checks from those original 233 women. Founding board member Belle Bear describes it as "staying true to our core values."

That early decision was a defining moment. From that day forward, Impact100 Pensacola knew that "staying true to our core values" would be the mantra they would repeat again and again. It has become a large part of who they are, and a large part of their success.

Those initial grants funded two transformational and sustainable projects that are still serving the community all these years later. One grant funded the formation of a brand-new health clinic offering medical and dental services free of charge to those in need. The other was awarded to Pensacola Habitat for Humanity and funded the creation of a Habitat ReStore, selling building materials, the profits of which resulted in fourteen families receiving homes in the first ten years.

Wildfires in Sonoma

The second story starts in 2017. Just as Impact100 Sonoma's renewal campaign was kicking off, massive wildfires swept through the area, devastating the community. Countless members had to evacuate from their homes, some returning to nothing but ash. At this defining moment, Impact100 Sonoma had a choice: give up or brush off their shoulders, roll up their sleeves, and get to work.

They chose the latter. The leaders knew they needed to be stronger than ever and come together to do what they did best: help their community. A newsletter was sent out to the membership amid the chaos of the fires, which provided next steps and an inspiring message from the co-presidents. Something really stuck with me within that message: "Recovery and rebuilding will take time, yet there is no doubt we will rebound stronger for it."

First, to keep Impact100 Sonoma alive and running, events were postponed and rescheduled. The grant application deadline was pushed back to give applicants more time to work on their proposals. To stay true to Impact100's core values, they emphasized that proposals did not have to include something about the fires. Applicants' grant requests would be given due consideration whether or not they were fire-related. In addition, the membership renewal campaign and the importance of the organization's role in awarding grants continued, especially during trying times when the community was under stress.

Furthermore, the chapter put together their resources of informal networks to provide help and support, which included providing places for evacuees to stay. One Impact100 Sonoma member coordinated more than fifty chefs from nearby to feed first responders and others. Cookbooks were donated at an event for those who had lost their cherished recipe cards due to the fires. Visa gift cards were collected at a holiday party to give to families in need throughout Sonoma. Furthering the giveback to the community, a group of about thirty members were organized to volunteer at a local food bank.

Through it all, Impact100 Sonoma's leaders supported, inspired, and led. They led with compassion and confidence. They stayed true to their mission yet flexible in the logistics to allow for maximum participation in their community, despite the horrific fires.

These defining moments truly show what something is about. It is in these moments our organization continues to commit to its core values of democratic collective giving. As Pensacola and Sonoma taught us, it is possible to find additional ways of responding to an immediate need while simultaneously honoring the Impact100 collective giving process. Maintaining rituals during these high-pressure moments keeps the roots strongly planted so the model can stand the test of time and continue creating a positive impact.

What can you offer your community during a crisis?

When a crisis hits our community, I believe it is natural to contemplate how we can help. This is especially true for any nonprofit organization that has time, money, and resources available to address the issue as it happens.

If unanticipated need arises in your community, an enormous burden of responsibility may weigh heavily upon you and your organization. In circumstances like these, the pressure can feel overwhelming, a challenge I know Impact100 chapters often face. As one of the most significant funders in their communities, our chapters often hear suggestions from individuals within the community for where we ought to deploy our grant dollars to help relieve the most immediate need.

In the heat of the moment, while emotion and fear run highest, determining our role can be challenging. I have found that understanding what our organization is good at and defining our role in the community is the first step in sound decision-making. In every community, there are typically experts at disaster relief funding. Impact100 is usually not the best equipped for this type of work.

In these times, we need to lead in other ways. Other community members often look to the leaders of Impact100 for guidance and to get their bearings. There are a variety of ways to respond.

Beyond money: more ways to support your community

- Use your voice as a leader to bring hope and perspective to the crisis. In a crisis, people need to hear a voice of calm and reason. Putting things in perspective and sharing information relevant to the issue can be hugely helpful.
- Point to the truth. Dispel rumors and falsehoods that often circulate during these times. Use your social media feeds to share vetted, truthful information.
- Give people a road map. Context is critical in times of crisis.
- Check your facts before sharing. We want to get it right.
- Use your voice to lead and help people to understand who we are—and who we are not—as an Impact100 organization. This can be a blog post or a message on your website or on social

media. You could do radio or TV interviews. Depending on the situation, you may write an opinion piece for your local paper.

- Be a resource. List trusted organizations that make a difference, and direct members there to get involved. Again, your social media feeds and website make spreading the word efficient.
- Understand your community feels helpless, but they want to help. Show them the way.
- Be a light in the darkness. Stay honest but positive.
- Increase communication. People want to hear from you.
- Stay calm and poised. Your temperament will reflect to your community.
- Lead through positive example. Don't share negativity on social media, personal conversations, email, or your website.
- Direct people to opportunities to give things other than money (blood, food, water, etc.).
- Stay true to who you are and to the commitments you made to your membership.

COVID-19

Impact100 Global was growing to meet the demand of the Impact100 community, had hired our first employee, and had rented our first office space on January 1, 2020. Our second employee joined us on February 10. By March 18, with the world in lockdown, we were each working from home and coming to grips with the changing world around us. Like everyone around me, I was adjusting to the new reality and unsure of what was ahead.

Not having any idea what might lie ahead, we did the best we could in the moment. Prior to the onset of the pandemic, I was sure that 2020 would be the year Impact100 Global reached complete sustainability. I had a team for the first time and a perfect little office in downtown St. Petersburg, Florida. We were poised to do so much, until the pandemic changed everything.

These "unprecedented times," as they were so often called, kept changing. The needs all around us grew exponentially, and our reality continued to morph. I found the guidance of Rabbi Yosef Kanefsky to be the right message for the uncharted territory of social distancing and shared it with Impact100 members: "Every hand that we don't shake must become a phone call that we place. Every embrace that we avoid must become a verbal expression of warmth and concern. Every inch and every foot that we physically place between ourselves and another must become a thought as to how we might be of help to that other, should the need arise."[12]

Pandemic pivots in Impact100 communities

Every Impact100 chapter faced new challenges with the onset of the COVID-19 global pandemic. As with so many individuals, we were all in the same storm, but our boats were vastly different. The age and location of an Impact100 chapter, coupled with the skill and experience of the leadership team, affected the response from the community. During these unprecedented times, every leader in each community did all they could to make the best use of their philanthropic resources.

---

12 Rabbi Yosef Kanefsky, "How We Must Reframe 'Social Distancing' to Truly Protect Ourselves & Others During the Coronavirus Pandemic," Your Tango, March 12, 2020, https://www.yourtango.com/2020332484/is-social-distancing-safe-during-coronavirus-pandemic.

When I spoke with leaders around the globe, their pain was palpable. To provide a safe space to explore solutions and share experiences, Impact100 Global began hosting weekly video calls we called "Chapter Chats." Largely structured as open forum discussions, we used this platform as a way to assure Impact100 leaders and help to guide and inform next steps as the pandemic widened. These conversations were well attended and provided guidance in real time, as the world seemed to be changing by the day.

Depending on the community, some Impact100 chapters carried out surveys and hosted conversations among their membership to determine the best way to support their local community. After taking a formal vote for approval from their membership, we saw some Impact100 chapters allocate funds raised in excess of $100,000 to their local COVID relief fund. This compromise solution provided some immediate relief to the community or assisted prior grant recipients with much-needed operating cash, while still offering the transformational grants of $100,000 to continue.

Impact100 chapters worked to increase communication to local members during this time. Zoom replaced in-person events, and as much as we all wished we could be together, we found that meeting remotely provided unexpected benefits, including record numbers of Focus Area Committee participation and Annual Meeting attendance. Many chapters created new opportunities for connection such as "Member Mondays" or "Finalist Fridays," and virtual wine tastings, book clubs, and coffee conversations flourished.

Some Impact100 chapters shifted their planned timing—either speeding up or slowing down the Impact100 process to allow the most involvement of both members joining and nonprofits applying for our funds. Despite the upheaval brought on by the pandemic and economic uncertainty, some Impact100 chapters stayed the course and did not make any adjustments to their funding practices or calendar. The flexibility of the Impact100 model was so beneficial, allowing communities to pivot—or not—to best serve and engage with the local community.

Where do we fit in?

As a community, we spent quite a bit of time discussing and considering the three stages of crisis response: immediate, intermediate, and recovery.

In the immediate stage, we focus on the urgent emergency need created at that moment. This is quite literally how to keep the lights on and serve the most basic needs, such as access to water, food, and shelter in a traditional crisis.

The intermediate stage follows, where organizations in the community take a quick breath while the lights are on and develop the next steps for the temporary or permanent new landscape. This is often the pivot—or reevaluation stage.

In the recovery stage the focus is on the act of getting back to what we would call business as usual. It is the rebuilding and regrowth stage when we can visualize our destination clearly but still need help getting there.

Funding after the recovery cycle begins is the path that keeps chapters most aligned with the original premise of Impact100. Depending on your viewpoint, this may be the most courageous. It is difficult to know what is best for a particular community and membership; by trusting the model, chapters will emerge stronger at the end of the crisis, as evidenced by the experience of the Impact100 chapters in Sonoma and Pensacola.

For communities with a strong disaster relief fund, Impact100 organizations can share the news and encourage members who have the financial capacity to contribute there. The role of an Impact100 chapter and leader is to serve as a guide to share the truth and shine the light on the resources available. Sharing news of nonmonetary resources that nonprofits and the communities they serve need can be quite powerful.

Connecting members with past recipients who have present urgent needs is also an effective way to respond in times of crisis. During the pandemic, we found this to be valuable. Many Impact100 members have the financial strength to do more—directly with the nonprofits they have come to know through the grant process that their chapter has funded or vetted.

Now more than ever

The economic, physical, and societal effects of the pandemic were constantly front and center in communities around the globe. This clear need encouraged some of our Impact100 chapters to grow their membership to new heights. The powerful leverage of combining the resources of hundreds of women, each donating $1,000, and then giving it all away in significant grants that stay in the local community was an incentive for more generosity and increased giving. During the 2020 calendar year, when the pandemic was at its height, we had a record-breaking nine communities successfully launch new Impact100 chapters while many others grew their membership numbers.

Phrases such as "Now, more than ever, we need your donation" resonated in communities who saw an increase in their grant pools. Those who were already giving stepped up with additional gifts, and those who were previously not philanthropic felt drawn to help. Even in the midst of uncertainty, loss, and fear, we saw generous people step up in Impact100 chapters around the globe.

Cultivating the skill of rethinking

I am a sucker for new technology. Every time I encounter the latest smartphone, tablet, or gadget, I would like to believe that it'll make me more productive, efficient, and effective. Thankfully, this desire is tempered by strong budget constraints.

Nevertheless, when news hits of a new gizmo, I am all in. I research the features and benefits to determine whether I will take the plunge to upgrade my technology. My logic is simple: If a tool exists to ramp up my productivity, it's worth the effort to assess its usefulness in my life and consider changing my current system. Can you relate?

I believe many of us react in much the same fashion when it comes to making a technology purchase. Yet when it comes to our deeply rooted life perspectives—some of which, if you're like me, we might have been holding on to since Reagan was in office—we're unwilling to budge on considering other views. Author Adam Grant thoroughly explores this premise in his book *Think Again: The Power of Knowing What You Don't Know*. In it, Grant uses science and story to describe the value of rethinking to all aspects of our lives, and his words ring true.

Including diverse thoughts and perspectives is a great way to assess how well your personal system is serving you. If you are concerned that changing your mind might be seen as weak or inconsistent, let me offer that intelligence is typically viewed as the ability to learn new things. From another vantage point, isn't intelligence also the ability to incorporate new information and therefore reach new conclusions as your data pool expands?

When I was in school, I loved the concept of a hypothesis, as it meant, simply, an educated guess. We were taught to first make our guess and then research to see if we were right or wrong. Our grades were not based on the guess, but rather, on the research. Sloppy or incomplete research led to a poor grade, regardless of the accuracy of the initial hypothesis. This kind of mental discipline brings about new inventions, initiatives, and solutions to the most vexing problems.

Just like the sea glass we admire when it returns from the ocean in all its new beauty, seeking out diverse perspectives and rethinking our own routines, systems, and assumptions can, over time, smooth our jagged edges and transform our ideas into wisdom.

Increasing Your Impact

The storms of life are inevitable. How we handle those storms defines who we are. To say it another way, when disaster strikes, we often have no way to avoid the situation and little to no warning about the event beforehand. We do, however, get to choose how we react. Our reactions dictate the ultimate outcome and can become our defining moments.

Storms have a way of testing our resilience. Sometimes, the storms of life can propel leadership and bring transformation. Nonprofits like the Livestrong Foundation and the Susan G. Komen Foundation were the outcome when a devastating cancer diagnosis hit too close to home. Many lives have been saved and millions of dollars invested in medical research in the aftermath of those storms.

When the storm comes and life feels out of control, look for the bright spots and the helpers. Decide what you can do and how best to respond. And then lead.

13

Generosity Is Contagious

No kind action ever stops with itself. One kind action leads to another.
Good example is followed. A single act of kindness throws out roots in all
directions, and the roots spring up and make new trees. The greatest work
that kindness does to others is that it makes them kind themselves.

—Amelia Earhart

I have always found walking the beach therapeutic, starting with those beach walks with Grammy when I was a little girl. I remember once, many years ago, when my husband, Rick, and I were on vacation, we did what we often do and headed to the beach for a nice, long walk. Some of our best conversations happened during these walks, and certainly beach walks can be a way to bring peace and clarity of thought into our busy lives.

On this particular day, we had started off on our walk with nothing more than a bottle of water to share along the way. Not far into our walk, I couldn't help but notice bits of trash along the shoreline.

Once I saw the trash, I couldn't unsee it, and it really bothered me. At first I thought, *I will be sure to pick those up on our way back.* I had not brought any kind of receptacle for trash. It only took a few more steps and a bit more garbage for me to realize that this garbage could not wait for my return trip. The trash was gross and needed to be removed from the beach as quickly as possible. I bent down and began gathering up the pieces of trash.

Unexpectedly, people began to smile and nod at us as we walked past. We heard murmured words of "thanks," "nice job," and "wow" from these strangers. One gentleman handed us a plastic grocery bag to help make our work a bit easier as he thanked us for caring. Others vowed to not walk past trash on the beach again and commented what a difference it would make if we all did our part.

The smiles and gratitude we experienced represented an authentic connection between strangers. It felt good. We smiled even as we picked up some of the most disgusting items we came across. Rick and I committed to carrying a bag with us when we walked the beach from then on, so we could be more efficient in our gathering.

The contagion—and chemical boost— of generosity

What we experienced is the contagion of generosity. By picking up the trash, I got a blast of a hormone and neurotransmitter called oxytocin. Oxytocin has a reputation as the "love or trust hormone" because it is released by the brain during moments of bonding. It floods a new mother's system immediately after giving birth. Thanks at least in part to this blast of oxytocin, the pain of delivery, not to mention nine months of carrying around however much extra weight, is all but erased the moment a mother first sees her precious bundle of joy. The pain just disappears and all you have in its place is love. The bond begins in that moment.

Of course, you do not need to have a baby to generate this bonding hormone. Hugging and shaking hands also produce oxytocin. Chemically, our body wants us to do more to produce this hormone. Once you feel it, your body will crave more of the activity that brings it on in the first place.

That day on the beach, as I was picking up trash, I got a shot of oxytocin too. When Rick saw what I did, he got a blast of oxytocin. At a subconscious level, his body wanted more, so he started picking up the garbage along the way. Our work inspired strangers who each received oxytocin and the urge to help in this way too. This cycle of behavior is how we are wired.

It turns out that cortisol, the hormone associated with stress, cannot coexist with oxytocin in our systems. The more generous we are, the more oxytocin floods our system, pushing out cortisol. The two chemicals have an inverse relationship, which means when we are stressed, it is more difficult to feel generous, and when we are generous, it is more difficult to feel stressed. The list of health problems that can be traced back to the presence of stress in our lives is myriad, and knowing the antidote is as simple and powerful as our own generosity certainly makes the case for finding ways to give back.

This helps explain how generosity is contagious. Generosity is good for us. It is a healthier way to live. When we give back, we feel good and we want to do more. As we give, the community gets better. Others see our work and want to join us. It becomes a beautiful cycle, a vortex of generosity. Impact100 is designed to expand this circle in bigger and bigger spirals, encompassing more and more people.

The spiral shell

When I imagine this spiral of generosity, my thoughts return to the beach and the beautiful spiral shells I collected with my grandmother. These shells can be enormous but start from humble beginnings. All it takes is a single grain of sand. The smallest act of generosity is enough to start the spiral in motion. We see this in communities around the globe as they launch a new Impact100 chapter. It begins with one person, then it becomes two, four, twelve, and before you know it, the entire community benefits as the spiral continues.

Doing good and being generous is a healthier way to live. Our bodies try to signal us to do more of this, but sometimes, due to stress and too much cortisol in our systems, we can't absorb these messages. To reduce stress, we need to be intentionally and wholeheartedly more generous. Instead of quietly steaming as the person in line in front of you adds her twenty-seventh item to the conveyor belt in the express lane of your favorite grocery store, smile kindly to the grocery clerk and pay attention to how you feel. In these cases, I often make up a scenario to explain the situation—for example, that the person in line is grabbing these items quickly so she can get home to an ailing parent, child, or puppy. It's hard to be cross with someone bringing food to a loved one, after all.

As Simon Sinek explains in great detail in his book *Leaders Eat Last: Why Some Teams Pull Together and Others Don't*, given that oxytocin and cortisol have an inverse relationship and cannot coexist in our systems, cultivating generosity is actually good for our health. The more oxytocin—and therefore, the less cortisol—the better! When we are generous, we have better health, we're better at problem-solving, we're more creative, we have more empathy, and we behave in a more ethical manner. Seniors who are generous feel more connected and experience a higher sense of purpose, while improving their health.

If you think about all the things that cortisol can do to your system, and then you imagine the oxytocin as the repair mechanism, you can turn wringing your hands about the problems you see in the news every day into the knowledge that you are a part of the solution—and your entire worldview changes for the better.

Gratitude can work the same way. Keeping a gratitude journal and writing down three or more things we are grateful for at the start and end of your day can truly change your life. I think the reason is because when we are grateful, we are being generous to ourselves.

Let's talk about money

Knowing that generosity is good for us and believing that we truly are biologically wired to give, we must also understand what we can do to raise generous children and encourage generosity in the people we know, regardless of age. Other than somehow exposing them to a life-changing brush with hardship, like cancer or a catastrophic natural disaster, the best way to ensure that children grow up into philanthropic adults is to supply them with adult role models who are generous. Taking our duty to model generosity a step further by talking with children about why, how, and to whom we give makes the lesson even more likely to stick.

One of the things I learned as a banker is that people do not like to talk about money, regardless of the state of their bank accounts. As parents, the topic of financial health is even more complicated. Wealthy parents are often hesitant to discuss money with their children for fear the children will become entitled and lose their incentive to work. Parents are fearful that a well-earned safety net might turn into a dreaded hammock for their offspring to rest comfortably in. Wanting their children to work hard and be productive members of society seems in conflict with sharing the truth about their financial security.

Alternatively, for parents who lack significant financial means, avoiding any conversations about money also takes center stage. These parents worry that letting their children know that money is tight would add too much stress or fear to their child's life. They want their kids to be kids—without the burden of responsibility of the family's financial struggles to weigh them down. They feel they must shoulder the financial burden in silence and plan to discuss money at some unspecified time when the financial picture is better for the family.

Over the years as a private banker, I have had the privilege to unpack the strategy of avoiding the topic of money with many families. Their unique circumstances were different, but my advice was always the same. Regardless of your net worth or sense of financial security, speaking in an honest, age-appropriate manner with your children about money is a benefit to all involved. Avoiding these conversations can result in feelings of shame, fear, or worry for your children, as they can likely sense whether you are being authentic. In many cases, they have already discerned the family's general financial means from context clues.

Like so many other important talks parents have with their children, talking about money can help you pass along values like education, hard work, and generosity, just like you eventually pass along your other valuables to your children. There are so many ways to involve multigenerational family members in activities to bring those ideas to life and make your priorities real and even tangible in meaningful ways.

You do not need to be a parent yourself to influence others to be generous; you simply have to be willing to share your story. Whether you share your experiences with young associates in your workplace, or with your grandmother, who never knew she had the capacity to make a difference, you can watch the seeds of generosity bloom in amazing ways by speaking up.

No ordinary piggy bank

When my kids, Stephen, Alex, and Hailey, were old enough to have weekly chores, they were given responsibility for small expenses they incurred, and they also began to receive a weekly allowance. I recall giving each child a dollar for each year of their age, so a five-year-old would receive five dollars and a seven-year-old would get seven dollars and so on. Upon receiving their weekly payment, all funds were carefully deposited into their piggy bank. This was no ordinary piggy bank, however; the bank my children filled had three separate color-coded sections: one for saving, one for spending, and one for sharing with others.

Each week, we divided the funds equally among the three sections with the understanding that each category had equal importance. As the coins clinked into each container, we talked with excitement about the toy they were saving for, their plans to spend money in the next week or two, and how they would share their hard-earned wealth. This bank was a vital part of their financial education. It put money into the context that it must be earned.

Connecting how many chores it took to gather each coin or bill before they accumulated enough to make that longed-for purchase made the item more cherished. They understood that money had a tangible, measurable value.

This bank did something else that was vitally important to the lessons of money I wished to instill: It made the act of spending, saving, and sharing our money all equal in importance. The simple act of dividing their allowance equally across the sections of their bank became a practical connection that each category was of equal merit. This is a lesson they have carried with them into adulthood.

Serving together

The same way I ensured my children understood the value of money, I was also intentional about providing experiences for them to understand the importance of helping others and giving. I wanted them to understand that not everyone had the opportunities they did.

I arranged for one of the kids' first giving experiences shortly after Thanksgiving one year. They had just begun talking about Christmas and what they hoped Santa would bring when I explained that their toy boxes and bookshelves were so full, there was no room to add anything more. I explained that many children didn't have toys and books. I asked whether they thought they had anything they would want to pass along to a younger or less fortunate child. Each one of the kids got a large black trash bag and began sorting through the playroom. They often conferred with each other, or with me, about what went into the bag and what stayed in the playroom.

When the task was complete, I quietly reached out to a local children's charity with a special request. I asked that when we came to donate the items, a staff member would meet us and specifically thank the kids and encourage their generosity. The resulting experience was overwhelmingly positive for the kids, and for me. The executive director spoke with each child individually, asking questions about a few of the toys being donated and expressing sincere thanks for each one's willingness to help children they would never meet.

From that day forward, we made similar donations a few times a year. After our initial experience, we simply dropped the items in the charity's receptacle, always remembering what we learned on that first day.

As the kids grew up, we volunteered by serving Thanksgiving dinner to families with special needs and later, to those who were homeless or financially unable to prepare a feast of traditional turkey, dressing, and all the trimmings. The act of serving others and making them feel special was not lost on my kids. They enjoyed the opportunity and were often the youngest taking part in these community meals. At one point, as we were serving the community Thanksgiving dinner, the kids were in middle school and were surprised to see children they knew from school seated at the tables. This made the needs of others personal, giving context and relevance to the needs of others.

These habits have influenced how each of our children lives today. I am incredibly proud to say that each child, in his or her own way, is authentically generous and powerfully compassionate. They truly feel a responsibility to leave the world better than they found it and seek out ways to help others.

Instilling the desire to give back and help our neighbors and those less fortunate is a skill that will serve your children well throughout their lives. You do not need to be wealthy to begin. All it takes is the willingness to take the first step.

Authentic, wholehearted generosity

Understanding how generosity can be like a spiral shell—as you give you also receive and the world gets better—might make some people think that giving is like a vending machine, and by leveraging this system they can get what they want by giving something that is easy to give. There is a catch, which is that your body knows the difference between wholehearted generosity and simply going through the motions for personal gain.

If, for example, you volunteer at the local soup kitchen because you know the CEO at the company you hope to work for volunteers, but you have no connection or affinity for the organization or the population it serves, you are not being authentically generous. That rewarding oxytocin? Nowhere in sight. The CEO you hoped to impress might feel good about your volunteering, but you won't, necessarily.

Do you remember the story at a Starbucks back in 2014 where in the drive-through line someone paid for their own coffee and then they gave an extra five or ten dollars to pay for the car behind them in line? From there, car after car kept "paying it forward" by giving money to the barista to cover the person behind them. Imagine this happening to you.

When you pull up, they would say well, guess what? The car in front of you has paid for your order today. Isn't that fabulous? Oh my gosh, it's not even my birthday! And what do you do? You pay for the car behind you. In the case of this particular Starbucks, this response went on for 457 cars! Four hundred fifty-seven cars paid for the person behind. So, you're thinking, who was 458? What happened?

Here's the way generosity works. Authentic generosity is when you give time, talent, or treasure with no expectation of receiving anything in return. What happened with that Starbucks is that the people at the window and the people in the cars, they sort of got in this rhythm, and it wasn't nearly as mind-blowing or exciting by the time they got to about four hundred. And so, when the guy (sorry, #458 was a man) pulled up, the barista said something like "Your coffee's already been paid for by the car ahead of you, just like the 457 people before you. Would you like to do the same for the person behind you and keep the chain going?" According to ABC News, the guy just said, "No."[13] Why did he do that?

The guy who said no and stopped the chain of generosity had his picture in the paper with a headline calling him the "least generous man in our community" or something similar. And he was publicly shamed for not continuing the "pay it forward" of coffee. If you take the time to read the article, do you know what that man did? He gave a $100 tip to the staff of that Starbucks. Talk about burying the lede, right?

He didn't do what was expected, but was he generous? Yes. Why didn't he give? He was later interviewed, and he said that he felt pressure to give to keep this going. But he didn't think it was impactful to pay for someone who was fully able and expecting to buy their own coffee, so why not do something significant for the people who were working there? I would say that that's generous.

Fundraising and the overhead dilemma

One facet of the Impact100 model we haven't explored deeply is the fact that 100 percent of our membership donations get pooled together into significant grants of $100,000 or more. The model is designed this way to ensure our members understand exactly where their donation is going. It is also because one of the barriers to giving is a suspicion that the rare examples of nonprofit CEOs making seven-figure salaries and riding in private jets at the expense of their mission is a widespread, systemic issue.

---

13   ABC News, "Meet the Man Who Stopped the 11-Hour Starbucks Pay-It-Forward: 'I Had to Put an End to It,'" WJLA, August 22, 2014, https://wjla.com/news/nation-world/meet-the-man-who-ended-the-10-hour-starbucks-pay-it-forward-i-had-to-put-an-end-to-it--106360.

Interestingly, this aspect of the model is often cited as a significant part of the reason many members join Impact100 in the first place. Members are also given the opportunity to become 110 percent members, giving $1,100, instead of $1,000, with the additional $100 going to help offset administrative expenses at the local chapter. This membership level has varying degrees of adoption, depending on the community and leadership.

Impact100 can serve as an entry point to philanthropy for many of our members. When members serve on Focus Area grant review teams, they are given an opportunity to more deeply understand what it takes to run a successful nonprofit, including the need for strong, paid staff. Through experience in Impact100, we find members expand their community involvement, increase their knowledge, and often seek out additional ways to make a difference.

Having personally worked on both the for-profit side of the economy and the nonprofit side, I am a strong believer that our industry needs better understanding and better funding for leaders and staff at all levels.

The notion that nonprofit leaders should make considerably less than their for-profit counterparts is not only ridiculous, it is detrimental. This paradox keeps talented leaders from pursuing nonprofit roles based purely on economics. Further, for many nonprofits, the key aspect of the programming they provide is the people who serve the community. Disallowing grant funds to pay overhead means this work cannot be expanded.

Giving is everyone's business

I was first introduced to Michael Chatman through his posts on social media. Michael's posts often echoed my own sentiments around generosity and encouraging community involvement. He had hundreds of thousands of followers on Twitter and hosted a weekly conversation using the hashtag #WhyIGive, which invited his entire network to give and to talk about their motivation, often creating enough volume of conversation for the hashtag to trend on the platform.

Michael reached out through a direct message, and we started speaking by phone about Impact100 and his work as senior vice president at the Community Foundation of the Ozarks. After learning about the Impact100 model, Michael wondered whether it would be possible to replicate the model in the rural Missouri communities affiliated with his Community Foundation. The problems that affect rural America are much different from those of bigger cities where Impact100 was thriving. Many of these remote communities are all but forgotten, and they deal with unique issues like geographic isolation, lack of public transportation, poverty, unemployment, and lack of internet bandwidth—issues that many of us take for granted in cities.

I traveled to Springfield, Missouri, in 2015 to meet Michael and visit some of the communities he had described. Since I had grown up in St. Louis, something about this visit felt like going home. I was also slightly nervous, understanding that not everyone you meet on the internet is who they claim to be. My nerves vanished when I met Michael. He is as generous and kind in real life as he appears on social media. He connected me with women who were eager to bring Impact100 to their communities. To date, three rural Impact100 chapters have emerged, representing more than two hundred women who together have invested more than $600,000 back into their neighborhoods.

One of those Impact100 communities is located just eighty miles south of St. Louis in the small rural community of Perryville,

Missouri. Becky Chapman, co-founder of Impact100 Perry County, was born and raised there. She describes Perryville as a small rural community of fewer than twenty thousand people. Becky tells me that Impact100 has been a game-changer for this community and the women in it.

One of the first grants awarded through Impact100 Perry County was to the Perry County Senior Services Center. The grant funded a new vehicle to expand their senior meals on wheels program, but what it really delivered is human connection. By adding an additional route with the new vehicle, volunteer drivers were able to spend more time with each client at their home—often the only human interaction these homebound seniors would have during the entire week. Their grants are relatively small when compared to the more than $100,000 grants in other communities, but they are transformational by every measure for these rural communities and the women who live there.

I share this story to show how powerful the Impact100 model is. It works anywhere, from rural to urban environments, around the world. The lives touched by a transformational gift are countless. Most importantly, great women come together and make a huge positive change in their own communities.

Increasing Your Impact

We are all leaders. Regardless of your job title, birth order, gender, or age, we have the power to influence others. Just as generosity and kindness are contagious, negativity can also spread like wildfire, if we let it. When we choose to set a good example, disrupt gossip, and do the right thing, we begin to change the world.

Intentionally sharing your story with others or inviting people to join you allows those good deeds, those moments of generosity, to grow as those who learn from you will replicate your actions, creating a vortex of generosity. The oxytocin your body produces when you are generous is a natural stress reducer. It also strengthens bonds among those who give with you or hear your stories of making a difference, because oxytocin is biologically linked to increased feelings of trust and affection.

14

Building Trust

> Everyone wants to be seen. Everyone wants to be heard. Everyone wants to be recognized as the person that they are and not a stereotype or an image.
>
> —Loretta Lynch

I've been a fan of Ernest Hemingway for most of my life. And not because I particularly loved any one of his books. It was because I considered him to be a neighbor. You see, Hemingway grew up hunting, fishing, swimming, and playing on Walloon Lake—the Northern Michigan inland lake where I spent much of my summers as well. This connection was enough for me to be interested in his work.

He has famously been misquoted as saying, "The best way to find out if you can trust somebody is to trust them."[14] This simple logic

---

14 The original quote is "The best way to make people trust-worthy is to trust them." See Ernest Hemingway, *Ernest Hemingway Selected Letters 1917–1961*, ed. Carlos Baker (New York: Scribner, 1981).

has always made sense to me. Sure, people give us plenty of reasons to be suspicious, but they also give us plenty of reasons to trust, so I choose trust over suspicion. I trust first. Then I pay attention. In most cases, my decision to trust gets reinforced with trustworthy behavior. When it doesn't, I am more cautious with that person until my confidence is regained.

Recognizing that not everyone is comfortable with this level of what one may call "blind trust," when I designed Impact100, I designed it to be fully transparent. Remember that one of the reasons women didn't get involved in their community or donate to nonprofits was the suspicion that funds would not be handled appropriately. By creating Impact100 with full transparency, my objective was to overcome any concern, build trust, and invite more women to get involved.

Importance of building trust

This system of transparency has served us well over the years. It not only draws members to the movement, but it also assures rising leaders take the mantle of responsibility in their chapter. When Impact100 was launched in 2001, it would have been impossible to predict the demands of giving more than twenty years later. Yet, as the movement has marched forward to the present day, the model has proven to be more relevant and resilient than ever.

Trends within philanthropy show giving circles are on the rise. In 2017, the Collective Giving Research Group published a report demonstrating that between 2007 and 2016, giving circles had tripled in number from 400 to approximately 1,600 giving groups nationwide. There is at least one giving circle in every state, and one in eight American donors has participated in a giving circle.[15] The sudden interest has produced a cascade of research that confirms what we've seen firsthand: Giving circles are about learning, building community, and empowering everyone to give back.

To understand why giving circles like Impact100 are growing in popularity, we have to examine the bigger picture. In 2021, the cultural consultancy sparks & honey, in partnership with the Morgridge Family Foundation (MFF), used its human and artificial intelligence platform to analyze the future trends in giving and identified five cultural shifts that will reshape philanthropy in the years ahead.

One of these shifts is the decline in societal trust across the board, from large institutions to individuals. Even before the pandemic, 64 percent of Americans said they lacked trust in specific individuals and government. The crisis of trust directly affects the world of giving. Sixty-four percent of individuals rate trust in a charity as essential before giving, but only 19 percent of individuals say they highly trust charitable organizations.[16] In a world of misinformation, polarization, and distrust, many donors feel helpless to make the right giving choice.

Against this bleak backdrop, giving circles have grown by 225 percent. According to the Future of Giving report, hyperlocalized groups can buffer the negative effects of misinformation and lack of trust by providing transparent, educational looks inside nonprofit

---

15 Collective Giving Research Group, "The Landscape of Giving Circles/Collective Giving Groups in the U.S.," 2017, 5–9, https://johnsoncenter.org/wp-content/uploads/2020/10/Giving-Circles-Research-Full-Report-WEB.pdf.

16 sparks & honey, "Future of Giving: Culture Forecast 2021," 64–68, https://www.sparksandhoney.com/reports-list/2020/9/14/futureofgiving.

institutions.[17] Giving circles that are structured like Impact100 provide an antidote to distrust by offering immersive learning about local issues, transparency about nonprofit interventions, and a sense of belonging within a giving community.

The Impact100 approach encourages members to dig deeper into local issues and selectively identify the best solutions available. Members are invited to investigate as much or as little as they like, and to share their findings with other members in their chapter. New givers gain confidence by working alongside more experienced philanthropists as they get firsthand exposure to the nonprofits in their community. While no member is guaranteed their favorite nonprofit will be awarded the $100,000 grant, every member has confidence that their options have been vetted and their vote counts equally in a transparent, democratic system.

Return on Impact research study[18]

In 2020, Impact100 Global collaborated with MFF to perform critical research into the work of Impact100 chapters. Although I have often said that Impact100 empowers women and transforms communities, I never had any data to back up those claims. MFF built a research team in order to get answers to these questions. We called the study "Return on Impact," or ROI for short, as we wanted to better understand the impact of Impact100. The lead researcher invited every active Impact100 chapter to participate, conducted interviews with chapter presidents, and surveyed chapter members and grant recipients. The aim was to evaluate how Impact100 affected members and communities.

---

17   sparks & honey, "Future of Giving," 78.
18   Meredith Dreman and Lihn Anh Le, *Impact100: Local Philanthropy Fueling a Global Movement* (Denver: MFF Publishing, 2020).

I was thrilled to be reaping the benefits of their efforts in compiling data on nearly twenty years of the Impact100 movement. Specifically, I wanted to empirically examine Impact100 member empowerment. Did members gain confidence in their giving during their time with Impact100? In order to answer this question, the researchers used Marc A. Zimmerman's Theory of Empowerment to define an empowered individual as the following:

> An empowered person might be expected to exhibit a sense of personal control, a critical awareness of one's environment, and the behaviors necessary to exert control. These different dimensions of Psychological Empowerment (PE) can be identified as intrapersonal, interactional, and behavioral components.[19]

The findings from this research clearly show the majority of Impact100 members demonstrate all three characteristics of an empowered individual: perceived control, critical awareness, and participatory behavior. Our members feel this way because the Impact100 process is intentional in democratizing philanthropy by ensuring every member has an equal say in our grantmaking. Here's a closer look at how:

Perceived control

To measure perceived control, the researchers focused on how informed members felt and how confident in giving they became. Members reported a strong understanding of the organizations they

---

19 Marc A. Zimmerman, "Empowerment Theory: Psychological, Organizational and Community Levels of Analysis," in *Handbook of Community Psychology* (Boston: Springer, 2000), 43–63, https://doi.org/10.1007/978-1-4615-4193-6_2.

gave to, as well as their role within the Impact100 chapter. Overall, data suggests that Impact100 members are well informed by the chapters, and actively exhibit perceived control over their own participation, their giving ability, as well as their donation's impacts.

Fully 93.1 percent of members confirm that their chapters clearly communicate the vision, mission, and goals. More than nine in every ten members said they are knowledgeable about how their chapter's grants have impacted the local community through the work of the grant recipients. Moreover, approximately 93 percent of members strongly agree or agree to the statement about making educated votes, which is "My chapter provides me with enough information to make voting decisions during the grantee selection process."

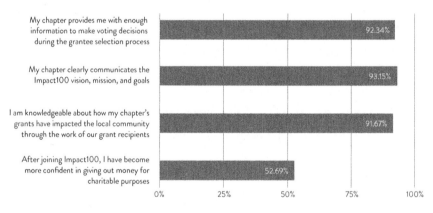

Graph 1: Proportion of members exhibiting perceived controls

Overall, slightly more than half of the members said their experience with Impact100 has improved their confidence when it comes to giving for charitable purposes. However, out of the 197 members who had never given a single gift of $1,000 or more to a nonprofit until they first joined Impact100, 70.6 percent felt *more* confident. This last point suggests that overall Impact100 has empowered its members to give more to the community—though the strength of that feeling of empowerment may vary depending on a member's prior experiences with giving.

Critical awareness

Learning about community needs is one of the central activities of giving circles. Therefore, to measure critical awareness, the researchers focused on the learning aspect of Impact100. In the survey, they asked members to share how participating in an Impact100 chapter helped them gain more knowledge about local community needs.

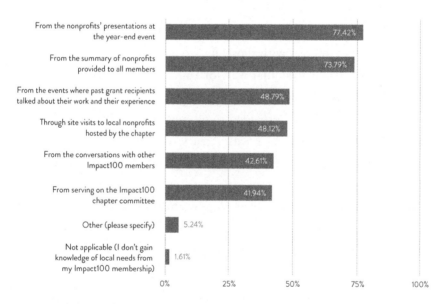

Graph 2: Proportion of members who gained knowledge about local community needs from their Impact100 membership

Graph 2 shows that fewer than 2 percent of survey respondents say they do not gain knowledge from being a member of Impact100.

We believe this represents the small percentage of members who are completely inactive within Impact100; they simply write their check and have no further involvement in the process throughout the course of the giving cycle.

Meanwhile, 98 percent of the respondents indicate at least one way their chapter enables them to learn more about local community needs. The most effective activity organized by a chapter, which enabled 77 percent of the respondents to learn, is the presentations by nonprofit organizations at the year-end event known as our Annual Awards Celebration or Annual Meeting. Qualitative data collected from the survey shows that members of Impact100 are particularly inspired hearing from the grant recipients, especially about how the grant has impacted their local community, and they wish for more opportunity to interact with those grassroots nonprofits.

The second most popular way for Impact100 members to learn more about the needs of their local communities is to read the summary of nonprofits provided to all members. Despite being all volunteer, the Impact100 Focus Area Committees (grant review committees) do a phenomenal job in synthesizing all the information from the grant applications to ensure members are well educated and informed. Interestingly, there is also evidence of shared learning among Impact100 members: One in every four survey respondents learned about local community needs by talking to other members.

Participatory behavior

In this research, participatory behavior is defined in three ways, namely continuing to give to Impact100, referring Impact100 to one's friends, and taking actions to provide further support to grant applicants whether they were awarded the grant or not.

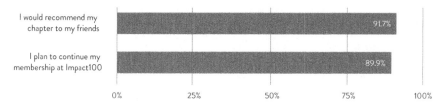

Graph 3: Proportion of members exhibiting participatory behaviors

Overall, almost 90 percent of respondents chose "agree" or "strongly agree" to the statement about their plan to continue their membership, and 91.7 percent would refer their chapter to their friends (Graph 3).

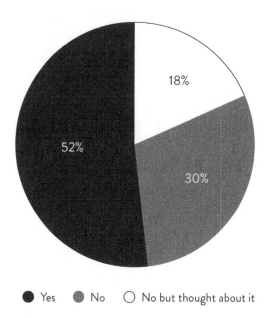

Graph 4: Proportion of members who take action to support nonprofit organizations they learn about through Impact100 (N=744)

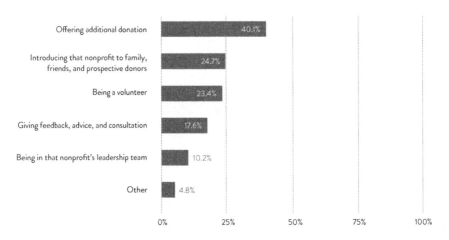

Graph 5: What actions beyond Impact100 do members take? (N=386)

Graph 4 shows that over 50 percent of the surveyed members discovered meaningful nonprofits from participating in Impact100 and took action to provide additional support. The support they provided was diverse, as shown in graph 5, even though offering additional donations to those nonprofits seems to be a dominant strategy. The research confirms previous findings that giving circles are highly engaged with grantees even beyond their direct financial support, through volunteering, contributing as board members of those nonprofits, and offering additional funding on their own.[20]

The fact that members of Impact100 proceed to assist the grant applicants—whether or not they were awarded the grants—shows a great potential benefit that nonprofits can expect just from applying for Impact100 grants.

---

20 Jessica Bearman, Buffy Beaudoin-Schwartz, and Tracey A. Rutnik, "Giving Circles: A Powerful Vehicle for Women," *New Directions for Philanthropic Fundraising* 50, no. 4 (April 2006): 109–123, https://doi.org/10.1002/pf.132.

Connections and wish lists

During this time that we at Impact100 were receiving so much data about how our members perceived the organization, I found myself thinking back to conversations I had with my dad back in 2001 when I was piecing together the elements of the Impact100 model. Throughout my life, he instilled real-time lessons about the importance of critical thinking. I remember watching TV with my dad during a political debate. At the commercial break, he asked whether I could recount what the politician had said, what it meant, and whether I believed him. I remember stumbling a bit, but basically could recount his point and said I did believe him. We talked about each candidate, their position, and the words they chose to convey that viewpoint. Together, we explored and questioned what each candidate had to say and why.

It was the first time that I remember feeling empowered to question the validity and authenticity of something said by an adult. It was a turning point that helped me to better understand the importance of understanding the situation at hand and not just blindly believing the way a person might present the situation. I respected my dad's wisdom and enjoyed these conversations. Sometimes his questions and our discussions swayed my viewpoints, while other times they gave me the platform to fully defend and further embrace what may have begun as not yet fully formed positions.

I had many powerful conversations with my father about the design of the Impact100 model. He was excellent at asking hard questions to challenge my thought process. One evening, as we discussed the idea that we would be giving big grants to only one to five applicants, while many worthy nonprofits would receive no direct funding from Impact100, we also discussed how our members might feel about the process. He understood that Impact100 members would become attached to the nonprofits and had the potential to be disappointed if their choice did not receive funding.

My explanation came in two parts. First and foremost, the Impact100 grant process would be transparent and thoughtfully communicated to each member. They would know before joining that they could only control their own vote but not the outcome of the entire membership vote. They would also understand that seeking to identify the grant recipient most deserving of a significant grant of $100,000 or more would mean turning down a large number of worthwhile organizations.

Second, we expected some members would make personal donations (or connect their well-resourced friends) to impressive nonprofits they learned about through their work with Impact100. To help facilitate a deeper connection between members and our Impact100 finalists vying for the grant at our Annual Awards Celebration, we asked each finalist organization to submit a wish list of smaller-cost or non-cash items and services needed. These wish lists were included in the packet of information members received upon arrival at the awards event. This concept was embraced immediately, with members giving more to the finalists as they reviewed the wish lists provided.

Often calling it "the impact of Impact100," the stories of nonprofits receiving donations, new volunteers, in-kind donations, and introductions to people supportive of their work abound in Impact100 communities around the globe. We consistently hear that nonprofits benefit greatly from the experience of applying to Impact100, even if they do not receive direct funding.

Additional funding

Following the 2021 grant cycle, Impact100 Oklahoma shared some wonderful news: The $190,000 in grants awarded by their membership was multiplied into $335,000 due to the generosity of their community! An additional $165,000 was given to support the nonprofit finalists.

The Impact100 Oklahoma newsletter put it this way:

As a finalist, Wings received $30,000 in membership money. Two weeks later an Impact Oklahoma member who was on the grant review committee donated $35,000 to be used as part of a matching challenge. Wings was able to raise the money needed to fund their project, Wings Serves Oklahoma Families. The ImpactOK member is now a weekly volunteer at Wings.

As a finalist, ReMerge of Oklahoma County received $30,000 in membership money. An ImpactOK member who heard the presentation at the annual meeting asked for a tour the following week. She was so impressed that she fully funded the ReMerge Pathway Project with a $100,000 donation! Yesterday, they celebrated the launch of the program as nine ReMerge mothers began training in their new family-sustaining careers in IT.

HALO Project took home a $100K grant this year. The following week they received an anonymous $30,000 donation from someone who heard the proposal and wanted to grow the reach of the Collaborative Impact Project. Instead of the original 5,200, they will now have the funds to reach 8,000 people the first year.

Representatives from all three programs thank Impact Oklahoma members for the opportunity to get on stage and present their projects. They expressed gratitude to have their stories and dreams heard by the membership and the community. This is why we do what we do.

This really is why we do what we do. As Impact100 members learn about the needs in their communities, and also the nonprofits addressing those needs, they want to do more. Sometimes the answer is additional funding. Sometimes it's much more than that.

Building lasting connections

Early in 2020, I had the good fortune of visiting Newport News, Virginia, the home of Impact100 Greater Peninsula. Several members shared their stories of people and nonprofits they supported after hearing about them through Impact100. At an event to kick off membership recruitment, I spoke alongside two nonprofit leaders who shared their stories of applying to Impact100 Greater Peninsula. Both told powerful stories of how Impact100 transformed their community, themselves, and the nonprofit they represented. Only one of the two was chosen as a recipient of an Impact100 grant.

First was Sanu Dieng, who was the well-spoken, poised leader of a nonprofit dedicated to serving women, men, and families fleeing domestic violence. Her nonprofit had received a transformational grant from Impact100 Greater Peninsula a couple of years back, but that was not the story she told. Instead, she shared that as a grant recipient, she connected to a network of savvy women in her local community. Her professional network had expanded to include several Impact100 members.

When faced with a sudden crisis—a building housing three families was deemed unsafe to live in due to a structural issue—she reached out to one of her Impact100 contacts looking for advice. She needed to quickly and confidentially re-home several families immediately. Her nonprofit didn't have the surplus cash on hand to simply rent new places for these displaced families, and given their circumstances, protecting their privacy while keeping them safe was vital. In one call, she was connected to another member of Impact100 who was in the real estate business. All three families were moved into their new, safe home in a matter of a few days, thanks to this generous network of women.

The next nonprofit leader to speak was a young man named Tony. His story did not begin the same way Sanu's did. Although he spoke eloquently and convincingly at the Awards Celebration, his nonprofit was not chosen as a grant recipient. However, that was not the end of the story for Tony. His personal story and the earnest, charismatic way he expressed himself left many Impact100 members eager to help him reach his goals.

Through his connections with Impact100 members, he received professional guidance and mentorship. He was introduced to people who could help him reach his goals and attend college. Although his nonprofit wasn't funded, he certainly received more than he could ask for simply by introducing himself and the nonprofit he represented to the impact of Impact100.

Increasing Your Impact

I am old enough to remember when President Reagan famously said, regarding a newly signed treaty with Russia, "Trust, but verify." His use of this old Russian adage served to bond him, and by extension, the United States, with Gorbachev and Russia as they worked to heal deep wounds of mistrust between our nations.

Since the inception of Impact100, I understood that this new concept would likely be greeted with a heavy dose of skepticism. Transparency has always been a key element of how an Impact100 chapter operates. In this way, each member has the opportunity to be involved and verify every aspect of our work. Decisions are not made in an ivory tower by a chosen few. Every member has the opportunity to help select our non-profit finalists, and every member has an equal vote.

15

Start Where You Are

> Philanthropy is not about the money. It's about using whatever resources you have at your fingertips and applying them to improving the world.
>
> —Melinda Gates

The trajectory of my life and career has not exactly been a straight or logical path that I could have planned. At the times I most thought my life was coming apart, it was really getting ready to come together in a completely new and different way. Now that so much hard work is in the rearview mirror for me, I can see the whole process more clearly, and it brings starfish to mind. You see, starfish have this amazing ability to reinvent themselves in different ways.

Starfish come in a variety of truly beautiful shapes, sizes, and colors. They are also inspiring creatures. You probably know that if a starfish loses an arm, it can re-grow that arm. But, like me, you may not know that if a starfish is attacked, it can *intentionally* drop an arm! Starfish can drop an arm to distract a predator, and the arm will regenerate in time.

It gets better: If part of the core or center part of the starfish is attached to the arm that is dropped, the arm can grow into an entirely new starfish! That's right—not just a new arm, but a whole new organism.

The ability to regenerate an arm or create an entirely new starfish represents a do-over of epic proportions. When I think about the regenerative powers of the starfish, it helps bring into focus for me the idea that we can all cast away whatever isn't serving us. We can cast away bad habits and excess baggage. We can cast away the old ways of doing things as a way to make room for us to grow new habits and new beliefs.

Ideally, that is what happens when we learn and meet other people who are doing the kind of work we wish we could do. The experience can help you realize that you are enough, that you *have* enough, and that the world needs what you have, whatever that is. When we come together, whether collectively in a formal giving circle or otherwise, we are joining hand in hand with others who want to see something happen. We want to see the building built. We want to see hunger solved. We want to see children with a backpack filled with the school supplies they need to be successful. Sometimes to be generous we have to let go of our limiting beliefs and of the fact that we don't feel we know enough or have enough or are in the exact right position to make change.

When we come together, beautiful things happen. I pride myself on being a continuous lifelong learner. I am always searching for ways to grow and learn. I do my homework. I seek out new lessons and try to understand what it takes to be successful. To determine how to reach a goal, I interview successful people I know, asking them what they did. Then I meld everything together and figure out how it applies to me—and how I can use it to better myself and the community.

When we operate with a growth mindset, seeking opportunities to learn new things and to learn from people we admire, we give ourselves the chance to create a better version of ourselves. We give ourselves permission to grow and change. Humility and curiosity are required to change in this way, as well as conscious effort. I have found that the results are more than worth the cost.

Taking the beach with you

I'm not so naive to think that *every* struggle and *every* trial has a happy ending, because unfortunately, I know that's not the case—and so do you. What I'm here to tell you is that each of us has a role to play. That role may change over the course of your life. Today, you may have little time. You may be active in your career or busy with your family. Perhaps you are involved in your community. Maybe you have lots of talent. You may even have a healthy checkbook. Use what you've got, where you are. If you're accustomed to always writing a big check and never rolling up your sleeves and getting involved, I would suggest you add the service component to your check writing. It will transform your life and make you a better donor.

If you are only giving your time because you feel you don't have enough money, don't wait until you're wealthy enough to give. That day won't come because you'll always have something else to save for. A rainy day will always seem like it's looming. The time to act is now. We need to be bold in our philanthropy, and we need to be bold in our generosity.

Choosing boldness means that we might make a mistake. And if we do, we need to forgive ourselves—we need to learn from the and pivot. Failure is not permanent, and mistakes are often the stepping-stones to better outcomes. We must be willing to risk a negative outcome to achieve a positive one. The more you give, the better you'll get at giving. The better you get, the better decisions you'll make, the better funding you'll provide, and the better mentor you'll be to those around you.

When we come together and talk about who we give to and why, where the most compelling needs are, and who has the most transformational solutions, we will continue to make better decisions. We will continue to hold those agencies accountable at a higher level.

Now is the time for each of us, in our own way, to give big, to be bold, and to make a tremendous difference in this world. The world needs you. Let your heart and your mind guide your next steps. You are the right person, at the right time, to do something generous.

Acknowledgments

I owe Carrie Morgridge a huge debt of gratitude for helping make this book a reality. Although I have long imagined writing a book "one day," that day came sooner than it would have thanks to a firm nudge in the right direction from Carrie. She knew much of my story and wanted it told, believing that in telling it, the Impact100 Global movement would appeal to people who would be compelled, as she was, to support this important work. Meredith Dreman and Barbara Brooks of MFF Publishing, along with the incomparable John Farnam, have been great collaborators and encouragers throughout the process. I am so grateful.

Writing this book has been a gift. To Rick, Stephen, Alex, Hailey, Brooke, and Jake, thank you for your patience with my long hours; your love and support mean the world. "Thank you" doesn't come close to expressing my gratitude for each of you. I love you more every day.

If a person is judged by the company she keeps, I am beyond blessed with smart, supportive, kind, loving friends. I am so grateful to the women who always have my back. This list is long but includes Tina, Joanne, Cynny, Carlie, Ilisa, Violeta, Kathy, Jennifer, Veronica, Jenn, Tandy, Stephanie, Martha, Teresa, Tonya, Amy, Toni, Denise,

Carrie, Cyndi, and Cortney. Each of you holds an important place in my heart. And to each of you, I owe a huge debt of gratitude.

There are also several men who support Impact100 and me in all they do. I am forever grateful to my father-in-law, Bob Steele, along with Howard Kaplan, James Boyd, and Nick Cianci.

The team at Greenleaf has contributed greatly to making this book the best it can be. Most of all, my editors, Amanda Hughes and Elizabeth Brown, have been a joy to work with. Their prompts, edits, and suggestions have made this a much better book.

Thank you to every Impact100 member, leader, grant applicant, and grant recipient around the globe. *You* have built Impact100 into the phenomenal force for good it has become. I hope I represented you well here in these pages.

Appendix

The Impact100 Model

This section provides a detailed explanation of how Impact100 is designed to work. Each facet of the model is explained and defined so even without any Impact100 experience, you will understand the premise of this powerful giving vehicle. When Impact100 is launched in a new location, sometimes local leaders will adjust some aspects of the model to best suit the needs of their communities.

One hundred women each donate $1,000

- For most people, a gift of $1,000 is a "stop and think" gift. For many of our members, it represents sacrifice and intentional budgeting to make a charitable gift of this size. That is by design. The effect is that each member feels connected to their giving—and to the transformational grants that are a result of their gifts.

- The year-one launch goal is to have at least one hundred women giving $1,000. The longer-term goal is to have at least five hundred women give at this level so the organization can give one grant in each of the five Focus Areas: Arts & Culture, Education, Health & Wellness, Family, and Environment.

- We value diversity. Impact100 seeks to include women of every age (minimum age of eighteen), faith, marital status, race, and ethnicity. We seek members who work outside the home in every profession and who are staying home with their families. This includes women who live in every neighborhood, women who are experienced givers, and women who have never given at this level before joining Impact100.

- One $1,000 donation equals one vote for how the pooled funds are to be used. If a woman can afford to donate $5,000, she cannot buy five votes; she can buy five years of membership or provide matching grant scholarships to women in need.

100 percent of members' donations go directly to charity in the community where the chapter is located

- Each Impact100 chapter defines their own geographic boundaries. This service area is determined by a number of factors, most importantly the pre-existing definitions of "local" defined by community stakeholders.

- The $1,000 donation goes directly into the grant-making pool, without any administrative costs taken from it.

- We ask (but do not require) women to give 110 percent to Impact100. When they give $1,100, the first $1,000 goes to the grant. The additional $100 (10 percent) goes to help cover administrative expenses of the local Impact100 chapter.

- Other ways to cover administrative expenses include gifts from members, family and corporate foundations, corporate matching gifts, sponsorships, in-kind donations, and donations from Friends of Impact100.
- Friends of Impact100 can be men, women, or companies. These are non-voting supporters who give in any dollar amount. Impact100 is run by volunteers. If paid staff is needed, those expenses are covered by special grants obtained expressly for that purpose (part-time database management/administration is the need most commonly staffed).
- Leaders serve two- or three-year terms in their role (maybe longer on the board, but in multiple roles). It is important that an Impact100 chapter's leadership changes routinely, especially the president(s).

Grants are distributed in increments of $100,000

- The minimum grant size is $100,000.
- For every increment of one hundred members, the organization gives an additional grant.
- The idea is to connect each member to these transformational grants. She should feel a part of something significant. There are other organizations that make smaller grants. That is not the role Impact100 plays in the community.
- This means some finalists will walk away without any grant money. We distribute wish lists from all of our finalists to our members and our friends.

- Nonprofits repeatedly tell us that they gain so much—even if they are not our grant recipients. The ripple effect is real, and we call it the impact of Impact100. Wish lists get filled and the organizations gain a network of passionate, connected women in the community.

Grant applications are solicited in five Focus Areas:

- Arts & Culture
- Education
- Environment
- Family
- Health & Wellness

Impact100 grant applications are reviewed and assessed

- Impact100 holds nonprofit information sessions where the grant process is explained.
- Grant applications must demonstrate the funds will be transformational and sustainable, with all proceeds remaining in the local community.
- Grant requests are welcome for any purpose allowable under the IRS rules. In other words, we allow requests for capital, endowment, operating, etc. The members may not vote to grant the request, but we try not to discourage applicants who need funds for these purposes.

- We do have financial thresholds for our nonprofits. They must be large enough to absorb a grant of $100,000 or more.
- We do not discourage larger nonprofits from applying for our grants.
- Nonprofits serving the Impact100 chapter's defined service area are invited to learn about Impact100 and apply for a grant.
- Each nonprofit selects the Focus Area they believe most closely aligns with the organization and the project/program for which they are seeking funding. They then rank each Focus Area from most relevant to least. The Focus Areas are designed to be broadly interpreted so that nonprofits addressing every need in your community may apply.
- Each nonprofit may only submit one grant application per grant cycle.

No time commitment is required, but participation is encouraged

- We know that member participation results in a better experience, but no time commitment is required. We are a no-guilt organization.
- Allowing women to design their own experience recognizes that we often have several competing priorities. And those priorities can shift quickly.
- The organization recruits members for the coming grant year during a specific period of time. Once the membership deadline has passed, the Impact100 chapter announces how much money they must give away to the nonprofits in the community.

Committees review applications, perform site visits, and choose a finalist

- Members who choose to be involved can serve on one of the Focus Area Committees (FAC).
- These committees review the grant applications. Members learn to vet the applications, ask discerning questions, and complete site visits.
- Members serving on FACs attest to being unbiased for or against each applicant and loyal to the stewardship of Impact100 members' funds above all else.
- Ultimately, the Focus Area Committees narrow their applicant pool to a finalist(s) that is presented to the voting members.
- All members receive an executive summary on each finalist along with an invitation to attend the Annual Meeting.

At the Annual Awards Celebration/ Annual Meeting, finalists present their projects and members vote

- All members receive an executive summary outlining each finalist and their grant request prior to the Impact100 Annual Awards Celebration.
- All members also receive wish lists from each finalist. These lists include in-kind needs and often outline other ways to assist the organization and its mission.
- Members who are not able to attend the Annual Meeting may vote by absentee ballot.

- At the Annual Meeting, finalists are asked to present for six to ten minutes with only a microphone and a podium. No more than two presenters are allowed for each finalist.
- No handouts, PowerPoints, or other technology is allowed. Animals and children under eighteen are also prohibited.
- We meticulously mandate a level playing field among our finalists.
- Members cast a confidential ballot that ranks the finalists in preferential order (first choice through fifth choice).
- Ballots are counted and validated by an outside CPA group or similar.
- The grant recipient(s) are announced.

Grants are awarded

- Grant awards are typically distributed over no more than twenty-four to thirty-six months. We execute grant agreements reflecting the circumstances and agreed-upon funding uses with each grant recipient.
- We maintain ongoing communication and stewardship between Impact100 and the grant recipient to ensure funds are used as described and agreed upon.
- Grant recipients must file timely reports as directed by Impact100.
- Grant recipients must wait two years before applying for another grant.
- Finalists who are not selected may reapply to Impact100 without restriction.

About the Author

Author photograph by Lisa Presnail

WENDY H. STEELE was recognized by *Forbes* in 2021 as one of fifty women over fifty who are leading the world in impact. She is the founder of Impact100, a grassroots global movement that has given away more than $123 million since its inception in 2001. After observing how her grandfather's banking career helped countless members of his community as she was growing up, Steele enjoyed a successful career in banking that culminated in a senior vice president role. Now a self-proclaimed "recovering banker," she has pivoted to focus exclusively on philanthropic work. From a young age, her family instilled in her the value of giving back with the intention of leaving the world a little better than she found it, leading Steele to believe that each of us has something important to give.

In 2020, Wendy was named a Distinguished Honoree of the Jones Prize in Philanthropy, an award that "honors someone who demonstrates the willingness to volunteer time, resources, and talents to improve the human condition, beyond themselves." Steele was also awarded the 2014 Jefferson Award for Public

INVITATION TO IMPACT

Service—considered the Nobel Prize of community service—for her work with Impact100.

Steele's work in philanthropy has been featured in several books, including *The Transformative Power of Women's Philanthropy*; *Women, Wealth and Giving*; *Creating a Women's Giving Circle*; and *The Right Sisters—Women Inventors Tell Their Stories*. PBS television created an hour-long documentary entitled *Impact100: Changing Lives, Strengthening Communities*, which highlights the work of Impact100 Pensacola Bay Area, the world's largest Impact100 organization.

Steele believes wholeheartedly in giving back to her community. She observes that there are two kinds of people: those who see the problems in the world and realize they can be a part of the solution and those who still need to be invited to the party.

About Impact100

IMPACT100 was founded by Wendy Steele in 2001 in response to feeling as though women's roles in philanthropy needed a new way to be expanded and encouraged. Wendy launched the organization with the goal of empowering women to see themselves as activists through utilizing large grants to make an impact within their communities.

By 2002, Impact100 received nonprofit status and donated its first grant of $123,000. In 2003, *People* magazine published a story about Impact100, and Wendy's idea quickly began to spread.

Today, her model has been replicated in cities all over the world and only continues to grow.

Learn more at Impact100global.org

Made in the USA
Monee, IL
24 April 2023